Growing Tomatoes

Everything You need to Know . . . and More!

By Nancy N. Wilson

Publisher's Notes

Growing Tomatoes
Everything You Need to Know . . . and More

By Nancy N. Wilson

Cover by <u>creative bella</u>

© Blurtigo Holdings, LLC
1st Edition – May 2016
Published in United States of America
ISBN-13: 978-1533178862

Disclaimer and Terms of Use:
The Author and Publisher have strived to be as accurate and complete as possible in the creation of this book. While all attempts have been made to verify information provided in this publication, the Author and Publisher assume no responsibility for errors, omissions, or contrary interpretation of the subject matter herein. Perceived slights of specific persons, peoples, or organizations are unintentional.

This material is designed to provide general information about the subject matter covered. The author and publisher are not engaged in rendering legal, financial, medical, or psychological advice. If expert assistance is required in these areas, the services of a professional should be sought.

Images

Tomatoes ©Leonardi – StockFresh.com

Thank You – ©Peterfactors - Fotolia.com

Caged Tomatoes ©Allison Fomich – Creative Commons

Cracked Green Tomato ©Erin Mahaney – California Cooperative Extension

Collars © Mindy McIntosh-Shetter – Tomato Casual

Bottom-end Rot ©NC State University Cooperative Extension

Early Blight ©Missouri Botanical Center

… for buying my book.
If you enjoy it, please take a minute and post a review
on the platform where you made your purchase

Growing Tomatoes
Everything You Need to Know . . . and More

By Nancy N. Wilson

For a complete list of my published books,
please, visit my websites
http://www.nancynwilson.com
http://www.amazon.com/Nancy-N-Wilson

Nancy N. Wilson

 Like

LIKE My Page on Facebook
https://www.facebook.com/NancyNWilsonAuthor/

Table of Contents

Introduction

You probably learned in grade school that the tomato is actually a fruit because of the way it develops on the vine. But, the majority of the world thinks of it as a vegetable, including me, so that is how we will primarily reference it in this book.

The tomato is the nation's most popular vegetable for home gardening.

Tomatoes can be found everywhere – in large rural farms . . . in the middle of suburbia . . . as plants standing obediently against houses in the city . . . and in containers on top of skyscrapers in metropolitan areas.

If you are interested in growing tomatoes, you are in good company. And . . . when you know what you are doing, it is not difficult.

I discovered early on that the hardest part of growing tomatoes was deciding on which varieties of the plant I should grow. I highly recommend that you stay with one or two; it is much easier.

The Tomato's History

Learning the story behind this legendary plant will make the time you spend fussing over your tomatoes more enjoyable.

The ironic part of the history is that tomato vines were once considered poisonous and no one ate them.

Tomatoes first grew wild in the South American Andes Mountains, but the native Incas did not cultivate the plants.

The pre-Mayan people of Central America carried the plants 2,000 miles, domesticated the "fruit" and began to eat it. They also named it - *tomatl* or *xtomatl*.

Unlike the tomato that we eat today, the early fruit was about the size of a cherry. In the South American tropics you can still find the original species.

Legend has it that Cortez, the 16th century explorer, transported the plant to Spain in the 1520s and it was cultivated in Italy (under Spanish rule at the time).

A Member of the Nightshade Family

Let's get back to the belief that the plant was originally considered poisonous. I find this very interesting (especially since I am a huge fan of the tomato).

Early botanists classified it as a member of the nightshade family, which includes many poisonous plants and is probably where the misconception originated.

Their logic told them that since it was a nightshade plant and nightshades are poisonous, the tomato was poisonous.

One of the old medicinal herbal books noted:

> **The tomato plant is more pleasant to the sight than either to the taste or smell because the fruit being eaten provoketh loathing and vomiting.**

Because of such notations and teachings, tomatoes were not eaten in England during the 1500s and 1600s.

In spite of all the "bad press," the fascination with them continued. Even though no one ate them, the American colonists took them to the New World – and raised them as ornamental plants. Even Thomas Jefferson grew tomatoes; but, he did not eat them.

Triumphant Culinary Debut

Finally a couple of centuries later in the 1820s, Colonel Robert Gibbon Johnson staged a tomato-eating event in New Jersey. He vowed to eat a basketful of tomatoes, and live to tell about it.

The event drew a huge crowd. Everyone wanted to witness his death by tomato. *(Guess they were starved for exciting events.)* This event was historic in a way because it would change the public opinion of tomatoes forever.

Johnson's doctor watched in horror after warning Colonel that he would, "foam and froth at the mouth . . . double over with appendicitis . . . if [the tomato] is too ripe and warmed by the sun." The doctor believed that Johnson was exposing himself to a "brain fever."

Of course, we know the outcome and Colonel Johnson lived to tell his grandchildren about the event. That was the beginning of the world's love affair with the tomato. It finally had reached its rightful place – acceptance as a food to be eaten and enjoyed.

Within a few years tomatoes could be found in local markets across the country. At first they were primarily used in preserves, pickles and catsup. People were still not entirely convinced that it was safe to eat them – and certainly not raw. They took precaution in cooking them . . . just in case.

Cookbooks of the day cautioned women to cook the tomatoes for a minimum of three hours to expunge the "raw taste" of them; but, the general public was getting closer and closer to accepting this new edible fruit.

The 1880 "Flower and Vegetable Catalog" of Rochester, New York, offered six different types of tomatoes from seed. In the late 19th century, different color tomatoes became available.

The legendary Burpee Seed Company offered a yellow tomato called the Golden Queen in 1888. In fact, they had approximately 22 distinct varieties to offer gardeners. Not a bad turn around for a fruit once considered deadly.

Finally in 1949, W. Atlee Burpee introduced the very first F1 Hybrid tomato. It was named the Big Boy and bred by Dr. Oved Shifriss.

This large, smooth tomato that ripened early was an instant success. Since then, the speed at which the tomato has been refined and bred . . . cultivated and harvested . . . canned and simmered into sauces . . . has been remarkable.

And we are all grateful – at least I certainly am . . . how about you?

Health Benefits

Current studies on its nutritive value have discovered that this delightfully delicious food is also an excellent source of vitamins and flavonoids (antioxidants that reduce the risk of cancer, heart disease, and other degenerative diseases).

The tomato has taken its rightful place as royalty in the garden and is also a major player in diets for people who are interested in a healthy lifestyle.

It makes me smile that a food once thought to be poisonous has become an important food for providing nutrients the body needs to stay strong and healthy.

Enough of all that! Let's move on to the important information . . . how to grow your own tomatoes and give you what the title promises: *Growing Tomatoes . . . Everything You Need to Know and More*.

In other words, you will find everything ***I didn't know*** when I started growing tomatoes - from a nice sampling of varieties . . . to how to grow them, fertilize them, harvest them . . . and many other points that you probably don't know you don't know.

But – no worries . . . I have written it all down for you and conveniently placed them in this little book. You will not have to chase the information down on the internet, or through books and magazines. It is all right here at your fingertips where you can study the information at your leisure in the privacy of your own home.

The Best Way to Use this Book

This is not a long book; so, you would be wise to read the book once all the way through. This will help you get a general sense for what is included. This is especially important if growing tomatoes is new for you.

Then, go back to the chapters that you need, depending on your current level of expertise.

We also recommend that you keep the book handy because as you continue with your adventure of growing tomatoes, you may discover that you want to consult this book again . . . and again. You may also find it useful to consult the book midway through your growing season just to make sure everything is moving along as it should.

If you purchased the electronic version, you may want to create a "shortcut" on your computer and place the book on your desktop or keep it in your Kindle Reader (with bookmarks in all the most important sections). With either of those two storage methods, the book is always only a mouse click away.

Grab yourself a cup a coffee and immerse yourself in a new, exciting hobby – one that takes you back to nature.

For me, a freshly-picked tomato from the vine, warm from the sun, eaten with a little salt, brings back wonderful memories. My mother was a great gardener and tomatoes were her among her favorites.

So, start right now and before you know it, you will be enjoying the fruits of your labor. (Sorry about the pun.)

Chapter 1
Choose Your Varieties

The first lesson of growing tomatoes is that all tomatoes are not created equal. It is important to understand this before you turn over your first shovel of dirt. If you are as impatient as I am and want to jump in without doing your homework, you will regret it.

The first step is to answer the following question:

Which Varieties Should I Plant?

When I first started, the original varieties I chose were not exactly a great match for my geographical region of the country – and the locations in my yard where I had planned to plant my tomatoes were all wrong!

It quickly became obvious that if left to my own devices, my first year of growing tomatoes would have been an utter and total disaster.

I had to rethink the types of tomato plants to put in my garden. So, you can, learn from my mistakes.

Before you dig . . . or even get your heart set on a must-have location for your plants . . . learn what the tomato plant likes and what it doesn't like.

Tomatoes are not really choosy plants. As long as you provide their basic needs, they do well and do not require a lot of fuss. In fact, you can have great success in your gardening endeavors merely by meeting the few basic requirements the tomatoes demand.

That is why the first chapter of this book, is all about the types of tomatoes available. If you do not choose the proper tomato for your intended use, your specific weather conditions, even your soil type, you may be disappointed with the results. I certainly don't want that for you.

When you are ready to buy your seedlings (or seeds), do not be afraid to consider buying several varieties of plants for the first year. This will allow you to test the process and see which ones do well in your garden and establish guidelines for the next growing season.

Growing tomatoes should never be a one-shot effort. It takes a little time to get really good at it.

(The First) Two Ways to Classify Tomatoes

Part of the wonderfulness (and confusion) you may experience when you first look into growing tomatoes comes from the hundreds of varieties from which to choose. It can definitely be information overload!

The varieties come in many sizes, plant types, the time at which they mature, how disease resistant they are and even their color. Making that initial decision can be a bit overwhelming.

Generally speaking, though, tomato plants fall into two broad categories. These two types are generally separated by plant height and cultivation requirements.

They are . . .

1. **Determinate**
2. **Indeterminate**

Not terribly exciting categories and even less exciting names! In fact, the names reveal nothing about the plants if you are not already familiar with them.

Determinates stop growing once the shoots set fruits. The flower cluster is at the growing point, which causes the plant to stop growing any taller once the fruit is set.

Indeterminate tomatoes, on the other hand, do not grow flower clusters at the end of the main stem, but alongside of the branches instead. The side branches and fruit continue to grow indefinitely, even after the fruit is set. They stop when hit by frost, insects, or disease. Most crop tomatoes fall in this group.

The older varieties of tomatoes are for the most part nearly always indeterminate. They produce not only an abundance of foliage, but they ripen flavorful fruit.

The only disadvantage of this category is that they mature rather late in the growing year.

Determinate plants ripen earlier, which can be a huge plus for some growers. It is interesting to note that when the determinate plants were first developed, they had two serious problems.

1. They didn't grow enough foliage cover.
2. The tomatoes didn't taste great.

The only factor in their favor was that they ripened early.

Those problems seem to have cleared up in recent years. Today determinate plants have better foliage, grow taller than ever before and actually ripen fruit that rivals many older tomato varieties.

Many farmers prefer determinates because they like to ripen their fruit over a short period of time. They plant rows in succession to ensure a steady harvest.

Growing tomatoes this way means that you don't have every tomato plant ripening at the same time and a glut of fruit in a short period and nothing two weeks later.

Plus, vines of determinate plants are easier to control and support during the growing season.

There is one additional category that I should mention:

Dwarf – Determinate and Indeterminate – These plants grow only a few feet tall (3- to 4-feeet), which makes them perfect for small areas or container gardens.

The **determinate dwarf** produces cherry-tomato-sized fruit all at once – and only one time per season. Many of the extreme dwarf tomato plants are determinate.

On the other hand, the *indeterminate dwarf* plants produce full-sized fruit all season long.

Two (More) Ways Tomatoes Are Classified

Another way to classify tomatoes is through the two terms **hybrid** and **open-pollinated.**

The **open-pollinated** plant refers to any variety that has the ability to cross-pollinate naturally with the ability to produce plants similar to the parents.

All heirloom tomatoes (any type that was grown before the 1940s), are considered open-pollinated.

A **hybrid** is the product of two types of plants that would not necessarily cross-pollinate on their own.

Hybrids were first developed after 1945 as the result of breeders searching for plants that not only produced more tomatoes, but also were disease resistant and more uniform in appearance.

Classification by Color, Shape, and Use

Several other ways to categorize these plants exist.

A common one is *classification by color,* which was a surprise to me. I always thought of tomatoes as being bright red! That may have been true in days gone by, but no longer.

Tomatoes come in orange, green, yellow, white, striped and even black (well, closer to a dark brown).

They are also separated into *classes by shape.* Traditionally, you say tomato and you think "round." But, that also no longer holds true for all tomatoes.

New shapes are appearing all the time. In a good produce section at the grocery store, you can buy cherry, grape, oblong, egg, pear and even flattened.

You can also choose varieties that are *classified by use.* Some tomatoes are best eaten fresh, right off the vine. Others are better tasting when you bottle them, make sauces out of them, or even allow them to dry.

Now that you are thoroughly confused, how are you going to decide which tomatoes to grow?

Let's dig a little deeper into this.

Let's start with varieties based on color and shape, starting with the best known - red and round!

Red, Round Tomatoes

These are the tomatoes you envision when you see yourself working in the garden. They are bright red, juicy and meaty . . . and they are traditionally round. These are the ideal choice for anyone who wants to grow "old fashioned" tomatoes.

Below is just a partial list of tomatoes in the "red round" category.

Better Boy - This is a hybrid that is also a determinate. It produces eight to 12-ounce fruits 72 days following transplantation. If you like a no-hassle slicing tomato, this plant is for you!

Big Beef, another indeterminate hybrid; it is also disease resistant. These tomatoes are usually no larger than 10 ounces, but, no smaller than eight ounces. The Big Beef takes 70 days from transplant to maturity.

Bush Big Boy is actually not as big as the name implies. The plant rarely gets taller than four feet. This hybrid indeterminate produces 10-ounce, blemish-free tomatoes. The fruit is seldom, if ever, smaller than eight ounces and are disease resistant. They take 70 days from transplant to maturity.

Cold Set is good to consider if you live in a cold climate because it can tolerate exposure to some frost. It is a determinate, open-pollinated plant with fruits that are somewhat smaller than the previous two types listed. They typically weigh from four to six ounces, and only 65 days from transplantation to maturity.

Costoluto Genovese, an Italian heirloom. It is an indeterminate plant whose eight-ounce fruits are not only juicy, but deeply ribbed. And as you may expect of a tomato of true Italian heritage, it has a strong tomato flavor. These plants crave heat and they take 80 days to mature from the time of transplanting.

Delicious not only describes a category of apples, it is also a tomato category that takes 77 days from transplanting to maturity. At the end of that period you have what many gardeners refer to as "the big one." The fruits of this plant usually weigh in at a minimum two pounds each! Now there is a tomato!

A Delicious Tomato is the world's record holder for the largest tomato ever grown: 7 pounds, 12 ounces. By the way, it is also an indeterminate heirloom plant.

Early Girl is a hybrid that *is not* a "late bloomer." Even though it is an indeterminate, it takes a mere 52 days from transplant to maturity. The size of these tomatoes generally ranges from four to six ounces.

Jetstar plants yield firm, meaty, low-acid tomatoes (8 to 9 oz.) that mature in approximately 72 days after transplanting. It is an indeterminate, but compact plant that grows 4 to 5 feet tall. Popular in the northern U.S. but harvest yield is excellent in areas like the South where there is a long growing season. Plants are also crack-resistant.

Oregon Spring is another tomato that thrives in the cold. This determinate, open-pollinated plant *contains very few seeds.* The fruit itself weighs in between seven to eight ounces and takes only 52 days from transplant to maturity.

Red Beefsteak produces large (14 to 24 ounces), meaty fruit with great taste that makes them perfect for sandwiches and salads. This indeterminate heirloom matures in the later part of the season – 90 days to maturity and is disease resistant. It is grown throughout the country, but a favorite in the Northeast.

Solar Fire is a heat-tolerant, which makes sense when you considered that it was bred at the University of Florida. This determinate hybrid produces large round fruits from seven to 10 ounces in size and is disease resistant. They also take 72 days after transplanting to reach maturity.

Stupice is an heirloom from the former Czechoslovakia that tolerates the cold well. It is an indeterminate with small fruit that weighs one to two ounces – and you will be enjoying the fruit 52 days after you transplant them.

Super Bush is a determinate plant that grows to heights ranging from three to four feet in size. The Super Bush does, indeed, produce *Super Tomatoes,* weighing eight to 10 ounces. The fruit is also disease resistant and goes from transplant to maturity in 85 days.

Colorful Tomatoes

Tomatoes of different colors are currently in vogue, and the popularity is well-deserved. The flavor of these tomatoes is equally as good as the traditional red tomatoes; plus, the colors can make an average casserole or salad a thing of beauty.

Here are just a few of the colorful varieties you may want to consider growing in your backyard.

Black Krim is a Russian heirloom. This indeterminate plant offers a unique, 12-ounce dark reddish-brown fruit. Not only is the skin dark, but also the meat of the fruit is dark. The temperature during the growing season impacts the color of the fruit – the hotter the temperature, the deeper reddish-brown hue of the fruit. The Black Krim is ready 80 days after transplant.

Brandywine has leaves similar to the potato plant, but it is a tomato plant of Amish origin that is ready for the table in 80 days. This indeterminate heirloom produces one- to two-pound fruits that have a pretty pink inside with a nice red color on the outside.

Many gardeners believe the Brandywine may be the most flavorful of all tomato varieties bar none.

You will also want to try Brandywine's "cousins" – **Yellow Brandywine** and the **Red Brandywine**. Why limit yourself to only one tasty variety when you can have three?

Cherokee Purple is a unique colorful variety. You would never know that you are growing a purple tomato because the outside is white (it is purple on the inside).

This is an indeterminate heirloom that produces 10- to 12-ounce fruit. It has a mild flavor, very few seeds, and a creamy texture.

Be flamboyant and try this with that Russian Black Krim to make a stunning black and white tomato salad.

Green Zebra is destined for greatness in the dish, "Fried Green Tomatoes." Both the skin and the flesh of this fruit are green -- even when fully ripe. The fruit of this indeterminate heirloom may only be three ounces, but are delightfully tangy and deliciously sweet.

Husky Gold grows to no more than four feet, but in spite of its size, it has a lot going for it. An indeterminate hybrid dwarf, it produces deep golden-colored fruit, about eight ounces in size. Only 70 days from transplant to table.

Lemon Boy lives up to its name – it is bright lemon yellow. It is a disease-resistant hybrid that takes 72 days from transplant to maturity and produces fruits that weigh about seven ounces.

Long Keeper lives up to its name. If you gather unblemished fruits before the first frost, they will keep up to 3 months in winter storage. This variety is a determinate, open-pollinated plant that produces 6- to 7-ounce orange-red fruit approximately 78 days after transplanting.

Sweet, Small Tomatoes

Grape, cherry and pear tomatoes are typically smaller and sweeter than other tomato varieties. They are wonderful for healthy snacks and in salads.

These are very productive plants – only one or two will provide all you need to keep your family happy.

The fruits tend to crack more than the larger varieties, so keep them well-watered and mulched regularly.

A sampling of small tomato varieties:

Golden Sweet is a small 1-ounce yellow grape tomato. The fruit has a mild, sweet flavor. It is an indeterminate, hybrid grape tomato that is easy to grow with no cracking and produces fruit 60-days after transplanting.

Patio is a perfect choice for the patio or containers because it is a hybrid, dwarf plant. Only 70 days after transplanting, you will enjoy the small red grape tomatoes. It is a determinate so the fruit will ripen all at once.

Sweet Million produces 1" to 2"red cherry tomatoes all season because it is a hybrid, indeterminate. It matures after only 60 days and offers good resistance to disease and cracking.

Tiny Tim tomatoes grow to only 18" in height which makes them perfect for containers. They are open-pollinated, dwarf plants that produce 1" diameter red cherry tomatoes in 60 days.

Window Box Roma is another 18" tall determinate plant that produces fruit all at once 70 days after transplanting. The name tells you the fruits are cylindrical-shaped small tomatoes that are great for sauce making.

Yellow Pear produces yellow pear-shaped fruits only 2" in diameter approximately 78 days after transplanting. It is an heirloom indeterminate that kids love.

Choices! Choices! Choices!

You must decide what kind of tomato crop will serve you and your family's needs the best.

We have barely scratched the surface of all the varieties of tomatoes from which you can choose.

So, how do you choose?

If you have gardening buddies, ask them which varieties they prefer (and why). They will love a chance to talk about their plants. Chances are, if you are visiting their home, they will even take you on a tour of their garden.

If you don't have any close friends growing tomatoes, seek out a good local nursery (a real nursery, not Home Depot or Lowes).

Many employees at quality nurseries are dedicated to gardening and plants of all types. Their business is gardening. If they can steer you in the right direction, it not only helps you, but them as well. Don't be afraid to tap their brain power and knowledge about everything tomato.

If you can't find the help you need when making your choices, look for the **_All America Selections_ _(AAS)_** winner label on the variety's label. A variety with this label has a pretty good chance of performing well in your garden.

Now that you are at least aware of some of the tomato varieties available and are mulling over which one(s) to choose, let's get excited about the actual act of gardening.

The next chapter talks about how to actually produce a garden full of healthy tomatoes.

Chapter 2
Growing Healthy Tomatoes

You are ready to get down to the real business – and true joy – of the hobby. It is time to plant your tomatoes, tend to them lovingly, and totally enjoy the activity of vegetable gardening.

But . . . first . . . as you read this chapter, take stock of what you have available and how you can take these ideas and plant them (pardon the pun) into your particular world.

As you go along, you should have some "aha" moments such as realizing that the corner in the backyard is the perfect place for a tomato patch. When that happens, you are off and running.

The first choice you must face is whether to start with planting seeds or transplanting seedlings.

A little hint . . . even if you start with seeds, you will still have to go through the transplanting process. For me, I love starting from seeds because it seems much more creative. I have done it both ways.

Answering the following question may make the decision a little easier: *How much time and energy do you have to devote to the project?*

Most novice tomato gardeners start with transplanted tomatoes; but, there are the adventurous ones who choose to grow their plants from seeds. It really isn't difficult, I promise.

Just in case you feel up to starting with seeds, I have included some directions below.

If not, you can purchase the seedlings and go from there.

From Seed to Fruit

Most people begin to plant their tomato seeds six to eight weeks before that long-awaited last frost of spring. The exact date, of course, depends on where you live. Once they have grown into seedlings, the tomatoes are planted. This should be about two weeks after the last expected frost date.

If that seems a little complicated (and frankly, anticipated frost dates drive me crazy); a good rule to follow is:

> *When you're growing from seed, you'll be taking the seedlings outdoors when the temperatures can stay in the mid-50 degree range both day and night.*

If you can estimate that date (possibly with a little help from the nurseryman), simply count back and do the initial sowing of your seeds about six to eight weeks earlier.

Seeds Must Start Indoors

Planting your seeds is an "indoor" job. This may sound like a no-brainer, but I wanted to emphasize the point because it is essential.

Begin with seed containers (which you can buy) and a well moistened, sterile seed-starting mix. Fill the container and create shallow furrows about ¼" thick.

Pencils or chopsticks are perfect for making these furrows. Drop the seeds along the bottom of the furrows in ½" intervals. Cover the seeds by gently pinching the soil together; then, water carefully.

If you are planting more than one variety, **be sure to label them. *You think you will remember where you planted each one; but don't trust yourself to do so.*** There are far too many other thoughts that will disrupt your memory – and you will kick yourself for not labeling.

Keep the container in a warm place – about 75 to 80 degrees. As soon as you see the seeds begin to germinate and the little stems start to peek out above the soil, it is important to give them a good, strong light source. If you do not have a good sunny window to set them in, place them below a florescent light.

By the seventh day, the seedlings should have germinated. You will recognize these by the "baby" leaves that develop. These are normally called *cotyledon* leaves.

A week later the seedlings are still rather tiny, but growing. The little guys should be a nice shade of green, which indicates they are getting enough light.

Around the end of the fourth week you will see the first real tomato leaves emerging right above those baby leaves you have been watching so closely.

Transplanting Seedlings into Individual Containers

Now, it's time to go back to work.

When the real tomato leaves have formed, you can transplant the seedlings into the larger individual containers you have selected for them (each container should be 3" to 4" wide – use biodegradable peat pots if you can find them).

By giving each plant its own container, you will ensure they have adequate room to grow and develop into healthy plants. .

Experienced tomato growers call this process **"pricking out the seedlings."**

Prepare your containers for their new arrivals. Make sure each is filled with a high-quality, well-moistened potting mix and poke a small hole in the soil.

This "pricking" step requires careful handling. Scoop up the entire soil ball from the bottom. An old fork is very useful in this process. Lift the seedlings gently with the fork, holding them tenderly by their cotyledon leaves.

If the roots of two or more plants have intertwined into a jumbled mess, not to worry; it happens all the time. Simply gently tease the seedlings apart, still holding the plant by its cotyledon leaves. If an occasional root breaks, it is OK; but, keep as many intact as possible.

Take each individual small plant and place it in its own container. Make sure each plant is inserted into the hole up to the base of the cotyledon leaves.

Each of these seedlings will grow new, strong roots. The plants, as you will soon see, will be sturdy and healthy. Once you have completed the transplant, water them gently to settle the little guys into their new homes.

The temperature of this new environment should be kept between 65 and 70 degrees until the true spring weather arrives.

Important tip: Once your plants reach 2½" high, start brushing your hands over the tops of the seedlings (10 strokes a day). This strengthens the stem and keeps the plants short and stocky, which reduces the transplant shock when you make the final transplant in your garden.

Hardening Off

When you know the move time is drawing near, acclimatize them to the out-of-doors. While still in their containers, move them outside into the sun – at first, just for short periods, two or three hours at most. Then bring them back inside.

After a week or so gradually increase the time they spend outside until they are in the full sun all day.

Gardeners call this process of gradually adjusting them to the outdoor growing environment "**hardening off**."

If you have ever grown herbs from seeds, you know exactly what I mean. The purpose of this slow introduction to outdoor weather is to avoid transplant shock.

When you are ready to transplant them, check their size. Any plant that is taller than six inches needs a few minutes of special preparation from you. See Trench-Planting for details

The next step is transplanting your seedlings, but before we get to that, let's talk about the soil for your new garden

Perfect Soil = Perfect Tomatoes

Whether you are a novice in raising tomatoes or a seasoned veteran, there is only one way to produce the best-tasting tomatoes in your neighborhood – **make sure they are planted in good soil.**

Yes! It does make all the difference in your final results. The right soil is the magic element in growing great-tasting tomatoes.

The soil should be slightly acidic. The pH balance should be between 6.0 and 6.8, according to *Organic Gardening* magazine. The soil should also contain a nice balance of calcium, potassium, phosphorus, and nitrogen.

Does your soil meet these requirements? Maybe – maybe not. If not, what can you do?

Working with Less than Perfect Soil

What if the soil in your yard looks more like a sandy beach than a fertile garden? First answer – don't give up. You can grow tomatoes in clay and sandy soil – **if,** you are willing to take the time and put in the effort to improve the soil.

The first step is to add compost. In fact, even if your soil looks pretty good, you should add one to two inches of compost.

According to Stephen Reiners, Ph.D., associate professor of horticultural sciences at Cornell University,

> *"This thickness of compost contains just about every nutrient a healthy tomato needs. Don't be afraid to toss a good shovelful of compost around your plants at least two and ideally three times a season."*

Some experts say that even three inches of compost is not too much, especially if your soil tends to contain either a lot of sand or clay.

Larry Bass, the extension horticultural specialist at North Carolina State University states,

> "You don't necessarily have to stick to pure compost. You may want to add some peat moss or other forms of organic materials onto the six to nine inches of soil."

The next step (especially if your soil is sandy) is to add lime and fertilizer. We will go over this point again later when we discuss the steps to lengthen your growing season, but this is an important step in the beginning, as well.

As noted above, the acidity of your soil is critical. Trying to grow your tomatoes in soil that does not match their pH requirements will slow their growth, produce a smaller yield, make them more susceptible to disease and insects, and reduce the amount of nutrients passed from the soil to the fruit.

It is important to note that the pH level of one area in your yard may not be the same as another.

You can test the pH level in one of two ways:

1. DIY with a pH soil-testing kit that can be purchased at any good nursery – they are inexpensive and easy to use.

2. Take a sample to the local county or university extension office's soil testing facility. (They will probably charge you a minimal fee.)

If you want to forgo the testing, and are not sure of the pH balance of your soil, simply add three-quarters of a cup of lime and a half cup of fertilizer that is labeled 8-8-8. The numbers designate the percentage of the three major nutrients all plants need for proper, healthy growth: nitrogen, phosphorous, and potassium

These three nutrients are always listed in the same order, so you never have to guess when you buy fertilizer. The first number represents the nitrogen content, the second is phosphorous and the third is potassium.

The addition of lime to your soil helps to reduce overall nutrient imbalances. This is particularly important when it comes to the calcium content. The lime also helps to control the blossom-end rot problem which can be a common problem with tomato plants.

Moving Your Little Guys Outdoors

Once the danger of frost is gone, it is time to plant these guys outdoors.

Two weeks before the final transplant prepare the soil for your final planting and then "heat it up." You can do this by covering the prepared soil with a dark plastic sheet. Pull it tight and cover the edges with soil. It will absorb the heat of the sun. This will jump-start your plants because the new roots will love the heat.

You will be amazed at how much they have grown from the first transplant to their individual containers to the time when they are ready to be moved to their permanent home "in the garden."

Just be sure not to get to anxious and move them too soon. When the temperature mark hovers consistently around the 55 degree mark, it is time – not before.

From Pot to Garden – Handle with Care

You have prepared the soil and warmed it to prevent transplant shock, it is time to prepare your garden the final planting.

Find out how large the mature plants will be for the variety you have chosen. Then, close your eyes for a minute and visualize the full-grown plants in the planting area. Make sure you allow enough room for them to grow without being crowded

They need lots of sunshine and space to breathe!

Plant them in rows that are not too close together. As a general rule the plants should be spaced a minimum of 1½ to 2 feet apart. Each row should have at least three to four feet separating them.

Use string tied to small stakes to keep the rows straight and spaced well.

Transplanting the Seedlings

Cloudy days or late afternoons are best for transplanting because the seedlings are less likely to dry out from mid-day heat and sun, and they will suffer less transplant shock that can come from severe temperature changes.

The prepared soil should be moist, but not soggy. Use a trowel to make a small hole in your garden for each seedling.

When planting most vegetables you want the holes to be deep enough that the transplant is the same depth in the ground as it was in the pot; but for tomatoes, you should go a little deeper.

Make the hole twice as wide as the root ball (or peat pot).

Unpot a seedling (unless it's in a peat pot) by tipping the container upside down, then squeezing or tapping it so the entire root ball will release.

NOTE: Handle the plants with care when transplanting. Rough handling can bruise and damage the plants resulting in slow growth or leaving them vulnerable to viruses or pests.

Handle the root ball carefully and settle the seedling into the prepared hole. The entire stem should be covered - up to where the leafy branches begin. Keep leaves free of dirt so the plants are not exposed to the many fungi and viruses that live in soil.

This process may go against your better judgment or may be different than the way you have transplanted other plants, but for the tomato plant it is absolutely necessary.

Scoop the soil around the plant and press it down firmly. Gently water the plant. Take your time and be thorough.

If you are setting the plants in biodegradable peat pots, make slits down the sides of the pots or gently tear the sides to enable the roots to push through. Also tear off the lip (top) of the pot so it doesn't stick up above the soil surface and pull moisture out of the soil.

The hole for each plant should be deep enough to allow the entire peat pot to be covered with a minimum of one inch of soil.

One of the things I did not realize when I first started was the importance of completely covering the peat pot – and quickly learned my lesson.

If the peat pot is exposed to the air it will rapidly dry the root ball and stunt the growth of your plant. In the worst-case scenario, it will even kill the plant, so be careful.

Give yourself a big pat on the back – you have completed the first phase of growing tomatoes. Congratulations!

Trench-Planting

If any of the seedlings are long and leggy, you have a decision to make. Some experts will tell you to toss them out because they will be weak plants prone to breakage with the slightest breeze. You can follow that advice, or take your chances. If you take a few extra precautions they could be fine.

You can use the *trench-planting method.* Dig a horizontal trench, not a hole, for each tall and leggy plant you have. Remove all the leaves from each plant with the exception of the top leaf cluster. There will be approximately four to five leaves remaining. (It will be fine, I promise.)

Then, (and this is the genius of this method), lay the plant on its side in the trench, cover the root system and bury the seedling up to the top leaf cluster. You should use about two to three inches of soil.

Next, simply firm the soil around and over the plant; but, do not press too firmly around the stem itself or it will break . . . And, there you have it.

Starter Solution

Once you have planted your tomatoes, you should make a **starter solution**. This solution will ensure that the young plants receive the proper fertilization during their early growth stages.

You can purchase a starter solution from your local garden center or nursery, or make your own by mixing one pound of a complete fertilizer (one that is labeled 8-8-8) in 10 gallons of water.

If that is too much for the few plants in your garden or mini-garden, make a smaller batch. Use three or four tablespoons of complete fertilizer in a gallon of water.

According to many experts, this is one area that the commercial offering is actually better than what you can make. The advantage of commercial mixes is their high phosphorus content makes them particularly effective for young plants.

When using these solutions (DIY or Commercial), keep in mind that more is not always better.

Never use more than one cup of fertilizer solution for one transplant. If you use too much solution, you may burn the root system. Dousing them with a super-strong, synthetic fertilizer can send them into a botanical version of shock, so use a light hand.

Supporting Your Plants

A common question is, "When should I add a stake or cage?" The answer is simple: the moment you plant it – or – as quickly as possible after planting.

To stake or to cage? That is the question. In general, staking a plant gives you larger, but fewer, tomatoes. So, if you like large tomatoes, the choice is clear: stake it!

Using Stakes

Buy a good six-foot stake at your local garden center and pound it into the soil to at least one-foot deep, approximately 3" to 5" from the actual plant.

Be careful if you have some trenched plants. Do not drive the stake into the root side of those plants – always place it on the other side.

You can use just about anything to tie the plant to the stake. Some gardeners use everything from cloth to a heavy string and even nylon stockings if you happen to have any of those laying around.

Using Cages

Image by Allison Fomich

On the other hand, you are more interested in quantity and not so concerned about size, you should cage your plants. If you are a do-it-yourselfer, these are easy to make.

All you need is a 5½ foot length of concrete reinforcing wire or even pasture wire. Form it into a cylinder shape with a diameter of 18" to 20".

Cut the bottom of the wire cage so the ends can be pushed into the ground. Set the cage in place over the plant, then drive two to three stakes around the *outside of the cage* to provide extra support.

Before we move on, take a minute, stand back, and let yourself feel good about your new gardening experience. You have earned it; but, there is more work to be done. You have only just begun a wonderful new growing season!

Side-Dressing Your Tomatoes

Side-dressing simply means applying fertilizer around (or "on-the-side") of the plants after they are growing. This practice is particularly important in gardens with sandy soils that do not hold nutrients well, and during growth spurts when plants require lots of nutrients. This gives them a little extra "umph" in nourishment to keep them going throughout the growing season.

Fertilizer applied at the time of planting will not supply enough nutrients for the entire season. Be careful, too much nitrogen in the beginning results in lush vegetative growth, but poor fruit production.

We will talk more about side-dressing in Chapter 3.

How to Fertilize

- Scrape mulch away from base of the plant (about 4-6 inches)
- Sprinkle 2-3 tablespoons fertilizer around the drip line of the plant. *Do not get fertilizer on the plant*– it will burn the leaves and stems.
- Gently work fertilizer into the top inch of soil with a small garden tool. Do not penetrate soil too deeply or you will disturb the plant's root system.
- Soak the plant with water to help fertilizer absorption into the soil.
- Scrap the mulch back around the base of the plant.

One pound of granular fertilizer will be enough to side-dress 10 tomato plants.

After the initial fertilization, apply another side-dressing when the first fruits are about one-third grown.

Apply again two weeks after picking the first ripe fruit – and again a month later. *(More on fertilizing in Chapter 3.)*

The Essential Ingredient - Water

Throughout the growing season, make sure your plants have enough water, which may require more than you think is necessary.

Water is definitely the essential ingredient if you want your tomato plants to produce the highest quality fruits. They need an even supply of water throughout the season – an irregular supply can cause problems.

A standard rule-of-thumb is that tomatoes need at least one inch of rain or irrigation water per week for steady growth. In hotter, drier parts of the country that can go up to two inches of water during the summer months.

Make sure that the soil around them is *soaked at least six to eight inches deep.* Check the plants once a week. If the soil is not wet that far down, you know it is a signal to water. Only water the plants when they need it.

Mulching Helps

In order to keep the soil moist, try mulching the soil around your plants. Mulch prevents the soil from drying out too quickly and can be extremely beneficial to the health of your plants, especially during the long, hot summer months.

You do not have to buy mulch (you can if you prefer, of course); but, something as simple as straw or even composted leaves act effectively as mulch.

Straw will keep the soil cool, so it is great for areas with extremely hot summers, but not suggested for areas with cool summers – at least not until the soil is warmed through and the plants are thriving – tomatoes love heat.

Types of Mulch

Shredded Leaves: Collect your fall leaves to use as mulch. They provide excellent protection from weeds and also increase moisture retention.

Grass Clippings: Spread grass clippings evenly around the stalks of your plants. The clippings mat together to protect plants and retain heat.

Straw: Golden straw and wheat straw are good choices. Stay away from hay, which is full of weed seeds.

Peat Moss: This decomposes slowly over the growing season, adding nutrients. Be sure to water your plants thoroughly before spreading the peat moss because it tends to suck moisture from the soil.

Black Plastic: Black plastic retains heat and usually increases tomato plant yield, but it is labor intensive and costly. It must be put down in the spring and taken up in the fall. Typically used most often by commercial growers.

Red Plastic: Used to retain soil heat and increase yield. Only use red plastic that has been proven effective for tomato growing. It is costly, but can be reused for several years.

Read more at Gardening Know How: Mulching Tomato Plants: <u>What's The Best Mulch for Tomatoes?</u>

For a Long Growing Season . . .

Harvest time is the delight of every tomato grower – novice or veteran. Many growers secretly dream of a growing season that never ends; some growers actually work toward this Utopian goal.

Some competing growers seem to take a perverse delight in seeing which gardener can keep his plants producing tomatoes the longest. Want to participate in this sport? It's not as hard as you think – and it is really quite fun!

Tips for a Longer Season

- **Give your tomatoes "elbow room"** when you plant them. Place the plants at least a full foot apart, as previously discussed. Plants that are scrunched together produce less fruit.

- **Plant with the stem half buried.** This may seem a little strange; but, it actually encourages the plant to produce more roots. As a side note . . . some experts advise against removing any of the branches, as well.

- **Try trench planting.** We have already covered trench planting; but, you may want to experiment and track your results. Plant some with their roots and some without (roots will eventually grow from the branches too).

- **Do NOT prune**. Pruning is a common process for most plants, but NOT for tomatoes – at least not if your goal is to produce lots of tomatoes. Pruning results in less fruit.

  If your goal is to extend your growing season as long as possible, then you definitely *do not want to prune.*

  However, if your goal is to produce bigger fruit, go ahead and remove the branches. We will discuss this in more detail in a later chapter.

The theory behind the "no-pruning rule" is simple. The more branches you leave on the plant, the more fruit you'll have at various stages of development. This protects you from losing your entire crop as the result of unexpected cold, wet weather.

- **Plant a variety of tomato plants.** That protects you from complete failure, which can result if you plant only one variety and that variety fails. It is unlikely with a variety of plants that they will all fail.

- **Plant both determinate and indeterminate plants**. This offers the potential of having not only the very first tomato in your neighborhood, but possibly the last one, as well. In the game of who-has-the-longest-season, that means you win!

That's One Cute Tomato

It is a fact of life that some people are blessed with beautiful genes. Others of us, well . . . not so much.

It is the same with tomatoes. Some tomatoes look beautiful hanging on the plants or stashed in a basket. Others – although every bit as delicious – simply do not have that same attractive presentation.

That doesn't mean that any variety is destined to grow up to be an "ugly duckling." You can make your tomatoes more appealing in appearance if you want to.

Below are some useful tips will help you become a creative gardener and grow beautiful tomatoes. They will also increase your harvest by extending your growing season. It just doesn't get any better than that.

- **Grow Your Own Mulch.** This tip will not help you with this year's crop, but it should do wonders for next year.

Hairy vetch, a type of legume which is grown to improve the quality of soil for other plants enriches the soil with anywhere from 60 to 120 pounds per acre of nitrogen. This is often used by organic farmers – aka ***fodder vetch*** or ***winter vetch***.

You can find this along the roadside – or you can grow it from seeds.

Hairy vetch jumpstarts several tomato genes into high gear. One of the most important is the gene that helps tomatoes resist fungal diseases. The other two genes are those that delay the time the fruit actually starts to be less healthy and encourages them to live longer.

It is easy to understand this step intellectually, but doing it can be a completely different story – but, if you choose to do it, it is worth the rewards involved.

Important Steps

1. **Sow your vetch crop in the fall.** If you have a large plot, be sure to mow or roll the vetch even before it blooms. This should be sometime in late May or early June. At the very least, you'll want to kill it before you plant your tomatoes. If you only have a small plot, simply pull the vetch by hand. Then lay it on the soil and keep it wet.

2. **Keep the tomato vines off the ground.** Many gardeners make their own cages with concrete-reinforcing wire bent in three-foot rounds. This not only keeps the vines off the ground where they are more vulnerable to collecting insects and other pests, but also helps the circulation of air, which helps decrease the incidence of disease.

Provide Adequate Calcium for Added Attractiveness

Another method to make your crop of tomatoes the most attractive it can be is by making sure they receive an adequate supply of calcium.

This mineral is absolutely necessary if you want to avoid blossom-end rot. With this disease, the plant develops a dry sunken end in place of the flower.

However, for the plant to be able to use as much of the calcium as possible, you must keep an eye on the soil's acidity levels. You must also water the area thoroughly so the mineral can be absorbed into the plant.

A good natural method of increasing the soil's calcium content is by placing crushed eggshells on the ground. Or, you can purchase dolomite lime.

Sunlight Is a Necessity

Tomatoes need a minimum of six hours of sunlight. This ensures that the ideal amount of photosynthesis takes place. It also helps to protect your plants from disease (and enhances the flavor – the hotter the sun, the better the flavor).

Before you plant, consider the need for sun. You will want to choose a spot that is not only sunny most of the day, but also an area in which the dew and the rain can evaporate from the plants quickly. That means exposure to some wind. In fact, do not hesitate to place your plants in an area that gets occasional gusts of wind.

Trellising Tomatoes

Whether you like your tomatoes big, fat, and juicy or prefer a bigger crop of smaller tomatoes, you will have to address the issue of how to support the plants. Right now they're probably either staked or caged. Both of these ways are good -- depending on the size and amount of tomatoes you want.

A third method of supporting the plants is trellising, which is used for larger garden plots.

There are many different types of trellis. There are directions online for a 3-Step Garden Trellis at: *MyHomeIdeas.com.*

OR – *you can follow the steps below to build a trellis:*

Step One:
Erect posts 3" in diameter or larger – 20 feet apart along your row of tomatoes that are spaced 12 to 18 inches apart.

Step Two:
Nail 10- to 12-gauge wire to the posts so that it is approximately five to six feet above the ground.

Step Three:
Nail a smaller wire to the posts 10 to 12 inches from the ground.

Step Four:
Tie a heavy twine between the top wire and the bottom one directly above each plant.

Step Five:
When the plants are tall enough, carefully ease the suckers, or branches through the bottom wire. As they grow, take the vine and again gently twist them around the upright twine.

Most farmers do this about once a week. The timing depends on how quickly your tomato plants are growing. Be careful to twist the plants in the same direction every time you do this.

Trellising will ensure that all your plants are up and off the ground, which will lessen the chance of their developing fungal infections.

NOTE: All dwarf plants need to be staked, caged, wired, trellised, or generally held off the ground to minimize rot and pest damage.

WOW! You are off and running on your new adventure. Let's keep the momentum going.

The next section will cover more about fertilizing your tomatoes, plus a discussion on weather-related problems you may encounter.

Chapter 3
Fertilizing and Maintenance

Growing tomatoes can be quite a satisfying. Not only are the tall plants beautiful and the ripe fruit picturesque hanging on the vine, they are delicious and nutritious, as well – always a good thing!

Make no mistake about it. If you want those big, juicy tomatoes to pop-up on the vines all season, you have to make sure the plants are getting enough food.

If you talk with experienced gardeners, you will hear them refer to tomato plants as "heavy feeders" – and they are right!

They like soil rich in organic matter and compost and respond well to side-dressing during the growing season.

When you experience the amazing growth of tomato plants and watch them grow from the stem – getting taller and taller – discover more branches every day, you will understand exactly how dynamic the plants actually are.

Each day you also see more leaves appear, as well as more blossoms. Then, the day comes when the first fruits are being formed. They begin to develop and the plant tenderly nurtures them until, before you know it, the fruits are ripening on the vine. It is Mother Nature at her best!

This amazing process requires a steady stream of water, and a good supply of vital nutrients.

More about Side-Dressing

We discussed side-dressing briefly before; but, now that you are a little more familiar with the planting process, the importance of this aspect of gardening should be sinking in.

You certainly do not want to "overdress," which will create blossom-end rot; but, at the same time you definitely want to apply enough fertilizer to keep your plants healthy.

If your soil is anything like mine – and millions of others out there – it is a good idea to side-dress at least occasionally

In case you have forgotten, this term is used to describe the process of applying fertilizer around the plants for that extra nourishment during the growing season. Generally speaking, you will only need to do this once or twice a year.

We recommended earlier in the book that you use fertilizer with a content of 8-8-8; however, many gardeners use other ratios as well. If you are interested in organic gardening, the experts in that field work with bone meal, dried manure, or even cottonseed meal. They get excellent results with those ingredients.

If you choose to go that route, keep in mind that the vast majority of natural fertilizers do not contain balanced ratios of the three major nutrients: nitrogen, phosphorus and potassium.

Manure, for example, actually tends to be quite low in phosphorus content. If you use this, consider adding bone meal along with it to provide your tomato plants with a complete diet. (Again, talk to a knowledgeable nursery man.)

Stay away from the high-nitrogen fertilizers. Common examples of these include urea, ammonium sulfate, and fresh manure. It is far too easy to use too much, which results in producing tall, dark green plants that bear very little fruit.

When and How to Side-Dress

That is an easy one! Side-dress your tomato plants the moment you see the fruit beginning to form. The ideal time is when the tomato itself is about the size of a golf ball. After that, according to some gardeners, you will need to side-dress about once every three to four weeks.

We talked about a fertilizer earlier and suggested a ratio composition of 8-8-8. You can also use one with a ratio of 5-10-10. If you use this, you will need a pound (about two cups). This amount will feed a 30-foot row of plants or about 20 plants. In smaller terms, this breaks down to about one and a half tablespoons per plant.

Spread the side-dressing in a 1" deep circular pattern around each plant. The furrow should be five to six inches away from the stem of the plant itself. Be careful! Do not get the fertilizer on the plant, the leaves, or the vines. It will definitely burn them.

Cover the fertilizer with one or two inches of soil – and you are finished.

Now – your job is to pour a large glass of iced tea, sit down on your back patio and wait for the next rain, which will start the process of taking the nutrients in the fertilizer into the root zone of the plants where they will gobble it up.

Pruning Your Plants

In many ways, the tomato plant is the victim of its own growth patterns. It grows so fast that it sometimes grows too quickly for its own good. A friend of mine calls the tomato plant a "solar-powered sugar factory."

In many ways he is right on the mark. For the first month of growth, most of the sugar the plants produce is directed toward the growth of new leaves, which causes them to grow rapidly. The average plant nearly doubles its size every two weeks.

Eventually, the plant actually manufactures more sugar than the single growing tip needs. This is the signal that the plant is ready to grow new branches and then flower.

Watch your plants carefully. Flowering usually occurs when the plants have 10 to 13 leaves and stand about 12 to 18 inches tall.

If you have not supported your plant through staking, caging, or trellising by then, this rapid growth could result in disaster.

The increasing weight of the fruit along with the many side branches forces the plant to actually lie on the ground, which is why it is important to support them as early as possible.

Once that main branch is on the ground, it begins to create even more branches. If not supported (and standing tall), one indeterminate plant can cover a four- by four-foot area with as many as 10 stems . . . that is not an exaggeration. PLUS . . . each of those branches, may grow to three- to five-feet long.

Think about the outcome of this kind of growth pattern! By the end of the growing season you would have an, impenetrable, disease-filled tangled mess of non-bearing tomato plants – definitely not your goal.

Pruning Indeterminate Plants

Because of this issue, some pruning is important. As a tomato gardener your goal is simple: *maximize the efficiency of photosynthesis and minimize the risk of disease.*

The way to reach this goal is to make sure that each leaf of the plant has sufficient room, is well-supported, and is not touching the ground.

When any part of a tomato plant is on the ground or forced into permanent shade, the amount of sugar it produces is greatly reduced. If a leaf uses more sugar than it makes, it will eventually turn yellow and drop off.

This is the only time your prune tomato plants – when it is necessary to keep it healthy. A plant that is both staked and pruned produces larger fruit two to three weeks earlier than one that is on the ground.

If your plant is properly pruned, all of its leaves will be reaching toward the sunlight. The vast majority of the sugar it is producing will be naturally directed to the developing fruit. Are you getting the sweet, sweet picture? In fact, if you have staked and pruned the plants properly, the only real competition for the sugar is the single growing tip.

A properly pruned plant produces large fruits at a steady rate until the first frost of the season strikes. The more stems allowed to develop the more sugar is diverted from the fruit and directed toward the stems. This will slow down your fruit production, but it won't stop it. In general, more stems will produce more, but smaller fruits, which develop later in the season

Pruning when necessary also has a beneficial effect on the health of your plants because the leaves of a pruned and well-supported plant will dry faster. This means that bacterial and fungal pathogens are less likely to spread.

Controlling the Growth of Side Stems

As your plant grows, the side shoots also begin to grow. These are called **suckers.** They form in the crotches, or axils between the leaves and the main stem. If you do nothing with these, they will grow, producing both flowers and fruit.

Suckers, if you watch your plants closely, appear in a very special order. They first start forming at the bottom of the plant, then work their way up the stem.

The farther up on the plant a sucker develops, the weaker it is because the concentration of the sugar decreases as it moves up the plant.

By contrast, the side stems appearing just *below* the first flower cluster are stronger and compromise the strength of the main stem.

Your goal is to have all stems on a multi-stemmed plant about the same size. However, the main stem should always be the strongest because it has to feed the entire plant.

Below are some tips and techniques for proper pruning to promote strong healthy plants.

1. Keep the side-stems free below the first fruit cluster. When the plant is trained to grow as one vine and left free-standing, it will naturally develop a strong main stem.

2. You can encourage such growth by trimming all the suckers.

3. Don't tie the plants to their supports until after the first flower appears.

Pruning Determinate Plants

These plants require practically no pruning. Simply remove the suckers below the first flower cluster. Easy peasy! This small amount of pruning will not affect fruit size or plant vigor. Do not do any additional pruning.

Indeterminate tomato plants, on the other hand, can have many more than just one stem . . . and, you do not want them to develop more than four stems.

Once again – fewer stems produce fewer fruits; but, they will be larger in size.

Another thing to keep in mind is that plants with fewer stems require less room. If space is at a premium, this is an important point to consider.

For multi-stemmed plants, allow a second stem to grow from the first node just above the first fruit. Then let a third stem to develop from the second node above the first set fruit. Continue this on up the plant.

The goal is to keep the branching as close to the first fruit as possible. This ensures vigor and health of the side stems. At the same time, they won't overpower the main stem.

Two Types of Pruning

1. Simple pruning

This is exactly as it sounds – simple! All you have to do is pinch off a branch.

The method works well when the sucker is still small and succulent. All you need to do is clinch it at the base between your thumb and index finger. Then just bend it back and forth. With very little effort, it will snap off. In the process it will produce a small wound. Do not worry about that, it will heal quickly.

DO NOT prune with a knife or scissors, if you can avoid it. Using either of these tools will leave a stump that can become easily infected.

There are exceptions to this admonition. Sometimes a sucker is just too tough and leathery and it will not snap it off with your hand. In this case use a blade, preferably a very sharp, retractable razor knife rather than scissors or a regular knife.

2. Missouri pruning

This is almost the same thing, but you pinch the tip – and only the tip – of the sucker, leaving one or two of the leaves. This can be advantageous because the plant has more leaf area for photosynthesis to occur. By keeping the leaves you are also protecting the fruit from getting burned by the sun.

Of course, this method also has a disadvantage; new suckers will inevitably develop along the plant's side seam. This only adds to your future pruning chores.

But Missouri pruning is sometimes a necessary step to take – especially when "things have gotten out of hand." When you are dealing with large suckers for example, it is better just to pinch off the tip of them than to cut the whole sucker. If disease should hit, it will be that much farther from the main stem.

Another reason for this is that it lowers the shock value to the plant. If the sucker is big, then your tomato plant will handle this small pruning better than cutting such a large part of it.

If you have never planted tomatoes before, you will be amazed how fast suckers grow especially during the hottest part of the summer.

You may feel a bit of sadness snipping them, but think about this for a moment . . . the side stems that start late in the season never produce good fruit. It is much better to prune them and allow the plant's energy to flow toward creating a higher quality of fruit.

The Season Is Moving Fast

Let's fast forward through the growing season.

The month before the first frost is rapidly approaching. It is always hard to admit and come to terms with the fact that the growing season has come and gone; but, it has and it is time to perform one last pruning. The fruit that is already on the vine needs every opportunity to mature.

Topping the Plants

- **When to Top**

Ideally, 30 days before the first frost in the fall. Of course, you can't predict this exactly, so give it your best guesstimate.

- **How to Top**

Remove all the growing tips from the plants – cut all the growing stalks back to where the previous growth stopped. This prevents any future growth in the stems.

- **Why to Top**

The purpose is to redirect the sugars and nutrients that travel through the stems. As the season draws to a close your plants are still bearing fruit that is not yet mature. If the stalks continue to grow, the fruit must complete for the "food" they need to ripen.

When the plants are topped, the competition ends and all the nutrients and sugars go to the fruit – so it can ripen fully.

This final pruning can make the difference between the last fruits of the season being hard and green destined to sit rotting in a bag somewhere or you and your family enjoying fresh tomatoes with your Thanksgiving salad.

Take note . . . go out and top those plants!

Weather-Related Problems

Sometimes the weather just doesn't fully cooperate with your tomato-growing goals. There is no need to throw up your hands and shout the world is out to get me (even though you may feel like it is). Learning to deal with weather-related problems can maximize your crop.

Blossom Drop

This is when the plants fail to set fruit. It is usually caused by extreme fluctuations in temperature.

Dry conditions and insufficient rain can result in poor pollination which, in turn, causes the flowers to simply fall off the plant without setting the fruit. This usually occurs when the temperatures dip below 55° F. or above 75° F.

In this case you may be able to outsmart Mother Nature by keeping your plants well-watered by deep watering once a week.

If the blossom drop is due to the *extremes in temperature*, there is not much you can do. You can take solace in knowing that once the temperature moderates, the fruit will indeed set.

Sunscald

Sunscald creates shiny white or yellow areas on the sides of the fruit that are facing the sun.

Eventually, this yellow area dries out and collapses. In place of the yellow spot, slightly sunken, wrinkled areas appear; that's when secondary organisms consider it an open invitation to invade the fruit, which causes it to rot.

Once your plants are affected, it is irreversible, but you can slow it down. You can either cover it with a lightweight screen or straw to prevent further damage, or you can pick the fruit and set it on kitchen counter to finish ripening.

Preventative measures include:

1. **Choose heat-tolerant varieties** if you live in high-temperature, sunny areas.

2. **Grow your tomatoes in cages** to provide good foliage protection.

3. **Keep your plants healthy** by taking care of diseases immediately so the foliage remains healthy. The lack of leaves may expose the fruit to the sun unnecessarily.

Cracking

Cracking is splits in the skin of the fruit around or from the stem.

There are two types of cracking:

Cracked Green Tomato by Erin Mahaney

1. *Circular Cracking* – around the stem.

2. *Radial Cracking,* which occurs from stem down toward the blossom end.

Some varieties are more prone to cracking than others. It is related to how well the skin stretches as it grows.

Cracking typically happens as the tomatoes ripen (reach maturity). It tends to happen if ripe tomatoes are left on the vine too long.

The varieties that are more susceptible may crack in the mature green stage, while the more tolerant varieties will crack at later stages, if at all.

When cracking happens early, the cracks will become longer and deeper as the fruit matures. Fruit on the lower trusses are more likely to have severe cracking.

Causes of Cracking

1. Heavier than usual rainfall or heavy irrigation immediately following a long, dry period. This encourages very rapid growth during the ripening period, which may cause the fruit to crack.

2. Exposure to extremely high temperatures -- greater than 90° F. – as well as direct sunlight.

3. Extreme variances in day and night temperatures.

4. Some varieties are more prone to this problem than others, especially plants with large fruit such as **Beefsteak Tomatoes**.

How to Control Cracking

1. Take care of your plants with correct pruning and leaf removal, which will prevent overexposure to the sun.

2. Take the necessary steps to prevent and control disease and loss of foliage.

3. Establish a good fertilizing schedule that will prevent overly succulent plants.

4. Do not over water! Water at regular intervals and adjust water quantities as needed. The goal is to provide an even amount of moisture to the plants.

5. During very dry periods, mulch your plants and water them regularly. The mulch will help keep the moisture in the soil for longer periods of time.

6. Monitor the nutrient content of your soil, and get advice on how to adjust it.

If you live in an area where cracking is a serious problem, it would be a good idea to select "crack-resistant" varieties of tomato, such as **Jetstar Tomatoes.**

Catfacing

Catfacing is scarred indentations found on the bottom of the fruit. The fruit puckers and develops deep crevices – sometimes so deep into the fruit that it is becomes inedible.

Probable Causes for Catfacing

There is a consensus among the experts is that one of the main causes is *cold temperatures* (below 50 degrees) during flowering and fruit set.

The causes of catfacing are not known for sure. But, it is believed that any disturbance to flowers or flower buds can lead to abnormally shaped fruits.

Disturbances such as environmental factors including insect damage and poor pollination and environmental factors may cause these malformations.

Some experts believe that low temperatures inhibit the normal growth patterns and prevent some parts of the fruit from developing correctly. The scarring results when the unaffected parts of the fruit continue to grow normally.

The bottom end of the fruit will develop brown scars, and in some cases cause the skin to "crack."

Erratic changes in moisture may also contribute to catfacing. Regardless of the weather try to keep your plants evenly watered throughout the growing season.

As previously noted, mulching helps the soil retain moisture when you are dealing with extremely dry weather.

If none of this seems to help and you live in a cooler climate, you may want to choose varieties of plants which are resistant to catfacing:

- **Early Girl**
- **Roma**
- **Heinz 1439**
- **Rutgers**
- **First Lady**
- **Beefsteak**
- **Ball's**

This problem occurs not only with tomatoes, but also with strawberries and pitted fruits such as peaches and apricots.

Leaf Roll

Cool, rainy weather may produce a distortion of the fruit called leaf roll, or leaf curl. It is exactly what the name implies - the lower leaves on the plant roll upward and become thick and leathery.

Luckily this condition has no effect on the plant growth itself or even fruit productions, nor does it require treatment.

And . . . that does it for now.

Chapter 4
Harvesting Your Crop

Your tomatoes are ripening and look beautiful on the vines. What are you waiting for? It is time to pick and enjoy!

I have no idea why, but some people hate to pluck the fruit from the vines – their natural home. Others hesitate because they are not sure when it is the "perfect" time to pick the tomatoes.

Actually, their fear is not without foundation. Tomatoes that are fully vine-ripened offer a better flavor than those that are picked early and ripened on the kitchen counter.

On the other hand, with some varieties (e.g. cherry tomatoes), if you do not pick the fruit soon enough they are prone to cracking.

To Pick or Not to Pick

End of the season is easy – once the *daytime* temperatures start to drop below 60 degrees, your fruit will refuse to ripen on the vine. That temperature drop is your signal to bring all the mature fruits inside.

But . . . what about other times throughout the growing season? How can you tell when a tomato is ready to leave the vine?

When you are picking only one or two for your family's meals on a daily basis, it is easy. You choose the ripest tomatoes you can find and leave the rest behind to ripen more.

Checking for Ripeness

1. **Check the color**. When it turns from the unripe green to its true color (usually red – but, as you now know, there are other colors), that is the external indication that your fruit is ready.

2. **Check the feel**. Ripe tomatoes are firm with a little "give" when you gently squeeze them. On the other hand, tomatoes that aren't quite ripe are rather firm and the skin is tight.

3. **Check the taste**. Pick one you believe is ripe and taste it. They are free – no charge. If it is not mature, you will know it right away because it lacks that tasty explosion of flavor homegrown tomatoes have. If it is overripe – it will taste starchy.

Flavor is the name of the game. Your goal is to attempt to leave the tomato on the vine for as long as you possibly can. While a tomato can change its color after you pick it, it does not affect the flavor, believe it or not.

Obviously, there will be times when you must pick the fruit prior to its fully ripening. When that is a necessity – *pick the fruit and some of the vine* and set the tomato on the windowsill with the stem facing up to avoid bruising.

You probably know this already, but if you don't, here's another important storage tip.

Don't store your tomatoes in the refrigerator!
It destroys the flavor and the texture of the fruit.

Storing the Fruit

You have an abundant harvest and more tomatoes than you need right at the moment. What do you?

The obvious answer is to store the tomatoes, but how?

1. Always wash and dry the tomatoes. If you are in the middle of the growing season and plan on eating the fruit within the week, nothing needs to be done. Your kitchen is your storage facility. Your windowsill, countertop, or a bowl works fine for this purpose.

2. If you know you will not be able to eat all the tomatoes within a few days, you need to search for a cooler storage place. For example, a cool pantry, or even a cool entryway will do. You will be surprised how long homegrown tomatoes will last just sitting around. It is a lot longer than those you buy from the market.

Ripening Green Tomatoes

Many tomato growers grew up in the era when the common practice was to place green tomatoes on the windowsill and allow Mother Nature do what she does best: bathe them in sunlight.

Today, the experts say this method is all wrong (blasphemy to many old-timers). The "new" experts recommend that tomatoes should be ripened in a paper bag. (What's going to happen when the paper bag disappears from the face of the earth?)

Their explanation is that while the light was absolutely essential to the growth and the setting of the fruit, once is picked it is no longer important. In fact, the best choice is a nice, dark place, like the inside of a paper bag. More than light, the ripening process requires humidity and temperature control. Tomatoes left to ripen on the kitchen countertop may dry out. Those placed in a plastic bag have a tendency to mold or ferment.

By placing your unripe tomatoes in a paper bag, it acts as a green . . . er . . . brown . . . house.

The Paper Bag: A Temperature-Control Unit

The ripening process requires an even temperature, and the bag effectively traps part of the heat from the day.

It also has another advantage. Tomatoes emit a gas call ethylene, which is common for most fruits as they ripen, but when you store the unripe, immature fruit in the bag, you'll stimulate the others around it to ripen as well.

Cool isn't it? Mother Nature has even built peer pressure into the process!

My mother used this trick with pears, and I understand the best fruit to place in a paper bag is the banana. They emit the most ethylene of all the various fruits.

If you are not convinced that the paper bag is a good idea, just keep in mind that for the ripening process you need heat. When push comes to shove, the best source of heat is the sun.

NOTE: There are differing opinions about this. See Tips from The Old Farmer's Almanac at the end of the book. You may want to try both options and make the decision based on your experience.

Late Season Pickings

When picking unripe tomatoes off the plant at the end of the season, be sure to pick the vine the tomatoes are on, as well.

Some people like to hang these vines upside down in a dark place, and believe it or not, the tomatoes will ripen. If it doesn't work, you can always serve "fried green tomatoes" – a favorite in the Deep South.

Canning (Preserving) Tomatoes

Your harvest will probably produce more tomatoes that you can possibly use – or give away. Throwing them away seems like a sacrilege, so learn to do what most tomato gardeners do – preserve them.

You have a variety of choices. Start with freezing them.

Yes, you can freeze them – whole, sliced, chopped, even pureed. They can be frozen, raw, or cooked, it is your choice. You can also freeze tomato juice and tomato sauce.

If you freeze them raw, you can then use them in any recipe that calls for a cooked tomato. You cannot substitute them for a fresh tomato. Freezing causes the texture to turn mushy.

NOTE: Since tomatoes should never be seasoned until just before you serve them, you definitely should not season them before you freeze them.

The freezing process will affect the seasoning, and it can go either way – the seasoning may be stronger, or it may reduce it completely. It is much wiser and provides tastier results to wait until you are ready to serve them.

Freezing Whole Tomatoes

1. Sort through your entire harvest.
2. Toss all spoiled tomatoes.
3. Select only the fully ripe tomatoes.
4. Wash them in fresh, clear water.
5. Dry by simply blotting them with a clean cloth or paper towel.
6. Cut the stem scar out.
7. Set the tomatoes on cookie sheets.
8. Place the sheets in your freezer. (Easy so far, right?)
9. When tomatoes are frozen, place them carefully in individual, heavy-duty freezer bags.
10. Seal tightly and place in the freezer. (Label and date)

Freeze Individually

It is best to freeze the tomatoes individually on the cookie sheets; and, then, place them carefully into individual small freezer bags. If you stuff them all directly into one bag, or other container, you run the risk of crushing them and having them freeze in clumps. This is not only bad for the fruit, it is also inconvenient.

When you're ready to use them, simply remove the number you need from the freezer. Peeling them poses no problem either. Run warm water over a frozen tomato and the skin easily separates from the fruit itself.

You can freeze peeled tomatoes if you prefer. Simply *blanch the tomatoes* (dip each tomato into boiling water for approximately one minute or until the skin begins to split) – the skin will easily slip off. Be careful not to burn your hands.

NOTE: No matter what others tell you, you do not need to blanch the fruit before you freeze it.

I personally prefer to peel them when I remove them from the freezer.

Frozen Stewed Tomatoes

Frozen stewed tomatoes is almost as simple as freezing them whole. There are just a couple more steps.

1. Peel your tomatoes. (Blanch for easy peeling)
2. Core and quarter them.
3. Place them in a large sauce pan.
4. Add other ingredients to taste (e.g. onions, celery, bell pepper).
5. Cover and cook until tender. (10-20 minutes)
6. Allow to cool. (This can be done by placing the cooking pan into a sink of cold water. Be sure to stir often.)
7. When cool, pack into freezer containers – allowing 1½" at the top for natural expansion that occurs during the freezing process.
8. Seal the container and freeze.

Frozen Tomato Juice

A delicious idea and so easy!

1. Wash tomatoes carefully.
2. Cut into quarters or eighths.
3. Place in saucepan and cover with water.
4. Heat to boiling.
5. Reduce heat to medium-low and simmer for 5-10 minutes.
6. Allow to cool.
7. When cool, press through a sieve or food mill to separate the pulp from the skin and seeds.
8. Pour juice into freezable containers – allowing 1½" for natural expansion when freezing.
9. Seal and freeze.

NOTE: You can add ½ teaspoon of salt to each quart for flavor. Don't worry, the freezing process will not change the strength of the salt.

Now you have some idea of when to pick your fruit throughout the growing season and after the final harvest, you know what to do with excess. As you can see, freezing tomatoes is quite easy.
In Chapter 5, we are going to look challenges you may face with diseased plants or pests.

Things happen, so it is important to be informed and prepared.

Chapter 5
Diseases and Pests

As with any kind of gardening, you must be prepared to deal with diseases and pests. There is no way around it; however, preventing problems is usually easier than curing them.

In researching prevention of problems with tomato plants, one of the best pieces of advice that I found regarding this subject comes from the Missouri Botanical Garden, <u>William T. Kemper Center for Home Gardening.</u>

Below is their list of ten strategies to help prevent diseases and other problems:

1. Although many heirloom varieties have better flavor than newer varieties, they lack disease resistance. Purchasing disease resistant [plants] can help, but keep in mind that disease resistance does not mean immunity. Preventive strategies are still important.

2. Disinfect tools, tomato cages, and stakes with a solution of one part bleach to nine parts water.

3. Rotate the planting location every three to five years.

4. Do not plant in cold soil. This weakens plants making them more susceptible to diseases and may stunt them permanently.

5. Do not crowd tomatoes. Good air circulation around plants is vital in keeping the foliage dry and preventing diseases.

6. Remove lower branches, leaving the stem bare up to the first set of flowers and then mulch (straw is a good choice). Many fungal diseases are in the soil or in bits of plant material left over from previous years. When it rains, fungal spores splash up onto the lower leaves, infecting them. The next time it rains, the spores from the infected leaves splash up onto the next set leaves. Unchecked the infection will spread all the way to the top of the plant.

7. Water in the morning to give the foliage time to dry out before nightfall.

8. Remove any diseased looking leaves as soon as possible.

9. If a spray program becomes necessary, use a fungicide (such as, chlorothalonil) alternated with a copper-based fungicide to help with bacterial diseases because even an expert can have difficulty distinguishing between fungal diseases and bacterial diseases. *Note: fungicides do not cure fungal diseases; they can only prevent them from spreading.*

10. At the end of every growing season, remove as much of the plant as possible from the garden and do not compost.

You may have noticed that a number of the things he suggested, we have already covered, but repetition often helps the information stick.

Unfortunately, no matter how hard you try, problems will arise; so, let's look at some of the more common ones.

Summer Weather Brings Challenges

Summertime is wonderful and the "livin' is easy," but, for the tomato grower, it means that you must begin to watch for insects.

There have been times when I wondered if there is a single insect that does not love tomato plants. If you are new at this, you may find yourself wondering the same thing; but take heart. There are solutions that do not necessarily involve harsh, chemically questionable pesticides.

Before you know it, those insects who think they have discovered easy livin' on your plants will be scurrying to find new homes – at least those that survive your attack, that is.

If insects aren't bad enough, there also seems to be a host of fungus that will also invade and damage your plants. While you know you should not take these attacks personally, sometimes it is difficult when you find your plants under siege from multiple directions.

This chapter will discuss the enemies waiting to ambush your crop of tomatoes. Being aware of the possible dangers, what can go wrong and what may be happening right now is a good start to solving the problems.

Invasion of the Insects

As I mentioned, there are many insects that love tomato plants. So… let's investigate the insects waiting to call your tomato plants home.

Hornworm

The most noticeable invader is the **hornworm**. When I say noticeable, that is exactly what I mean, They measure 3" to 4" long – you can't miss them.

Hornworms are actually caterpillars whose favorite menu includes the leaves at the top of your plants. Because they are so big, you can see them easily and pick them off. There are also some insecticides that will keep them at bay, if you prefer.

Cutworm

Another caterpillar, although not nearly as huge as that hornworm, is the **cutworm**. In fact, these guys are tiny, but powerful! They will feed on your plants at night while you are sleeping and once they begin, there is no stopping them. It is not unusual for cutworms to actually eat through seedlings right down to the ground.

I know it sounds horrible; but, it doesn't have to be. These menacing little creatures can be stopped with a few simple steps.

Preventing damages from these creatures begins with placing collars around your seedlings. So, let's look at how to do that.

Collaring Your Tomatoes

Don't panic. This is much easier that it sounds. You can make the collars yourself using paper, cardboard, paper cups, aluminum foil, or even a disposable aluminum pie tin.

Image by Mindy McIntosh-Shetter at Tomato Casual

Home Guides at SF Gate offers the best directions I could find on How to Stop Cutworms on Tomato Plants by creating collars for your seedlings.

1. Cut 3-by-10-inch strips from stiff cardboard, such as a cereal box. Bend each strip to form a circle, and tape the strip's ends together to keep the circle intact.

2. Slide a cardboard circle over the top of each newly planted tomato seedling. Push the bottom edge of the circle into the ground. Cutworms usually won't climb over such a collar to reach tomato plants. Cut the cardboard collars off the plants once the plants are 12 inches tall and their stems are too thick for cutworms to bite.

3. Sprinkle 1/2 tsp. of cornmeal around each tomato plant. Before they reach the tomato plants' stems and leaves, cutworms will eat the cornmeal, which results in their death.

4. Place moth traps, which contain floral lures, around the tomato plants. These traps destroy the moths that lay cutworm eggs, and they prevent problems later in the growing season.

5. Inspect the tomato plants with a flashlight at night if you suspect cutworms are causing damage. Pick off the cutworms by hand, and drop them into a bowl of soapy water to kill them.

6. Clean up the garden bed promptly at the end of each growing season, and dispose of all old plant material. Cutworms overwinter in dead plant material. Till the soil two weeks before planting so all cutworms buried in the soil are exposed and killed.

You can click visit the website at http://homeguides.sfgate.com/ to read the full article.

Nematodes

Another common tomato pest is the **nematode**. If your children ever watched the cartoon, "Doug," you know that he was always searching for that elusive, legendary nematode. Until I took up gardening, I thought it was a fictitious creature. Now I know better . . .

Nematodes are, in fact, among the most dreaded pests ever to plague tomato plants. There are nearly 20,000 different species of these worms around. *Talk about a potential problem!*

Experts say that literally billions of these microscopic worms occupy every acre of fertile earth. Given that, it is amazing that they don't give the growing tomato more problems than they do.

The good news is that within the 20,000 species some nematodes are actually beneficial because they help control other pests. For example, one species can help you fight fungus gnats or even flea beetles.

Gardeners, as a rule, do not discuss nematodes; but when one does announce that he has them on his plants, everyone scurries to ward off the onslaught. Every gardener within earshot know exactly what he means and soon you will too if you stay with this hobby long enough.

Let's look at a few of these tiny worms:

The first one is the **root-knot nematode**. This species delights in invading crops, and seems especially happy with causing bumps or galls that actually interfere with the plant's ability to acquire its necessary vitamins, minerals and other nutrients. These nematodes also disrupt the process of photosynthesis.

Your plants are more prone to being attacked by this species if you live in a warm climate with a short winter.

Getting rid of them is tricky. Their attack begins several seasons before you realize they are there. That fact is a vital piece of information.

if you grow vegetables along with your tomatoes, you can deter the pest by rotating your crops. Do not plant the same types of plants in the same place year after year. When you rotate your planting, it throws off this particular pest and they find it difficult to entrench themselves in one place.

However, do not plant another nematode-vulnerable vegetable or relative of the tomato plant such as peppers, eggplant and even potatoes. You are welcoming them with open arms if you do.

However, you can plant okra, peas, beets or squash as part of your rotation process.

If you find that your plants are infested with nematodes, you may want to switch to **nematode-resistant varieties of tomatoes.**

You can tell if a particular variety is nematode resistant because it's marked with an N. This may not eliminate the problem entirely, but less damage should occur.

Juice-Sucking Insects

Enough about nematodes, let's take a look at another type of pest, juice-sucking insects. There are several of these; so, let's begin with **whiteflies**.

This pest loves to suck the yummy plant juices. Much like the aphid, whiteflies leave behind a sticky residue, or "honeydew," as many growers describe it. To make the problem worse, the residue can become the ideal host for **sooty mold**.

To find out if your plants are infested with whiteflies, just disturb the leaves of affected plants. If they are present, you will see the whiteflies rise up from them. Don't bother with insecticides; they do not work on this little creature. They have developed a resistance to all of them.

There are only a couple of solutions to this problem that I am aware of. One is to lay out yellow sticky traps to monitor and suppress infestations. Another surprisingly effective method of dealing with them is simply by hosing down the plants, especially if you use something called a *bug-blaster*.

This is an attachment for your garden hose, designed to produce an intense multi-directed spray. It has no problem actually reaching the undersides of leaves. You'll be amazed at how well this works!

You can also fight fire with fire. In this case fight insect with insect. Stage your own "Ultimate Fighting Contest" - Insect Edition. To help control the invasion of whiteflies, you can release natural predators.

In this case, ladybugs, lacewings or even whitefly parasites; sometimes you just have to be sneaky like that.

Next in line – **aphids**. I am sure you have heard of these pesky little creatures. They attack a variety of plants, including tomato plants. These guys also love to suck the juices from your plants. They are sneaky; they like to hide on the underside of the leaves.

You can easily identify these insects by the sticky honeydew they produce. It is not uncommon for newbie tomato-growers panic when aphids strike, but there is no reason to do so. They can be easily eradicated with an insecticidal soap.

Another juice-sucking insect that attacks tomato plants is the **psyllid**. These guys seem to attack in cycles. Some years they are a bigger a problem than other years.

It is important to catch them as soon as possible. When the leaves start to yellow and curl, there is a very good chance psyllid are present.

If left unchecked, the damage they do will eventually slow the plant's growth and prevent the production of fruit. Insecticidal soap works well against these psyllids, as it does with aphids.

Next, we have the **flea beetle**. They are a little different. They are not suckers, they are chewers. They chew small holes in the leaves. After their feast the leaves look like someone has taken a tiny shotgun and shot your plant full of holes.

Bottom-end Rot

This has come up several times already, which means it is important to give you more information so you can combat it when you see it. But, even more important, so you can avoid it altogether.

Blossom-end rot is a weather-related problem and is very serious. Sadly, it doesn't strike only tomatoes. It is also a danger to peppers and eggplant.

This disease strikes the very first fruit of your crop, which is a horrible experience. If it is your first crop, it will probably be a very disheartening experience.

When it strikes it can be devastating to your crop. Some gardeners experience losses of up to 50% (or more) of their crop.

You can recognize blossom-end rot as a small, water-soaked area at the blossom end of the fruit. This can appear at any time; but, it usually appears when the fruit is still green or just as it begins to ripen.

As the lesion (as many horticulturists call it) develops, it grows, becomes sunken, and changes color. Eventually, it turns black and leathery.

If your crop is stricken badly enough, the disease may creep up onto the fruit, making it flat or even concave.

Once the lesion forms, other problems develop from that, which can completely destroy the fruit.

Blossom-end rot is a result of low calcium content in the fruit itself. Your plant requires calcium for normal cell growth. When the plants do not get enough, the tissues of the cells break down, causing dry, sunken lesion shown in the image above.

Causes of Calcium Deficit

Drought or fluctuations of moisture in the soil can create a calcium deficit. Water shortages slow the transportation of calcium to the plant and cause poor uptake of calcium through the stem. Dramatic fluctuations of moisture disrupt the growing and absorption process of the plant.

The type of soil can also be a factor. Acidic, sandy, or coarse soils often contain less calcium. Even though there may be sufficient calcium in the soil, it may be in an insoluble form and unusable by the plant. Soils with high phosphorus content are particularly susceptible to creating insoluble forms of calcium.

Another factor in calcium deficiency is due to improper or overuse of fertilizers, such as excessive usage of potassium or nitrogen fertilizers. *Too much nitrogen* results in the plant growing too fast to absorb the calcium it needs.

Solutions to the Problem

There are four things you can do to reduce your risk of blossom-end rot.

1. Maintain the proper pH balance in the soil

This alone will go a long way in keeping your plant healthy. The pH should remain fairly constant – around 6.5. We discussed how to check your pH balance in an earlier chapter.

This level can be maintained through the process of **liming**. Liming will give the soil more calcium while at the same time increasing the ratio of calcium ions to the other competitive ions in the soil.

2. Use nitrate nitrogen

Make sure your fertilizer nitrogen is of the nitrate variety. The other is called ammoniacal nitrogen; this type may actually increase your incidence of the disease. The ammonium ions in this nitrogen reduce your plants' uptake of the calcium

Along these same lines, you'll also want to avoid over-fertilization as part of your standard side-dressing early in the year.

3. Avoid fluctuations of soil moisture.

You can do this by ensuring that you mulch or irrigate your plants – or both. As a rule of (the green) thumb (noted previously), plants generally need about one inch of moisture a week either from rain or through irrigation for their proper growth and continued healthy development.

4. Don't apply calcium to the leaves.

This is a useless practice. The amount of absorption that actually occurs during this method is negligible. Plus, the calcium needs to be absorbed through the stem, not through the leaves.

Fungus Problems

Early Blight is a fungus that is carried through the soil and hides out in plant residue. It can start when you bring transplants home. It affects the foliage, stems and fruit of your tomato plants and is a problem that every tomato grower faces eventually.

Missouri Botanical Garden

It produces dark spots with concentric circles on the leaves, with the older leaves being affected first – starting at the bottom of the plant and moving upward. The area around the spot may also turn yellow.

Once the leaf is touched with early blight it will probably die prematurely. This in turn exposes the fruits to the sun, which can result in sunscald.

To help manage this disease, remove the affected plants and remove all fallen garden debris.

Although this is not classified as a weather-related disease, wet weather can worsen the problem. Plants that experience stress are also more susceptible to the blight. Spraying with a copper or sulfur spray may help prevent the further development of the fungus.

Gray leaf spot affects the leaves of tomato plants – and only the leaves. Like early blight, this disorder strikes the oldest leaves first. Small, dark spots begin to form on both the top and bottom surfaces of the leaves.

The grayish-brown spots grow fairly quickly. After a while the centers of the spots crack and fall out. This stage lasts only a short time after which the remaining leaves turn yellow and fall off – once again, exposing your fruit and adversely affecting fruit production.

As soon as you notice the problem, remove all affected plants immediately. Remove the fallen garden debris as well. Warm, moist conditions make this disease worse. Anything you can do to give your plants drier conditions will help.

Just as there is early blight there is . . . **late blight**. This not only affects the leaves of your plants, but the fruit as well. This disease is rather infamous.

It is the disease that caused the Irish Potato Famine (1845-1852). It destroyed the potato crop and decimated the population because about two-fifths of the people were solely reliant on this cheap crop for survival.

A primary trait of this disease is the swiftness with which it spreads. Cool, wet weather encourages the growth of the fungus.

You can recognize it from the greasy-looking, irregularly-shaped gray spots on the leaves. Around the spots you will sometimes see a ring of white mold. This mold ring is particularly noticeable in wet weather.

The spot ring itself eventually changes into a dry, paper-like texture. The blackened areas may then appear on the stems as well. The fruit is not left unscathed either. It develops large, odd-shaped greasy gray spots as well.

The fungus that causes late blight can survive a cold winter; and, as mentioned above it can ruin potato crops, as well. If your plants contract it, you must remove all tomato debris and clean the area thoroughly. Also do the same with your potato debris, as well. if you have any.

If you believe your plants have this particular disease, contact your local extension service immediately. They will help you to make a positive identification.

Southern blight produces a white mold on the growing stem near the soil line and dark, round spots that appear on the lower stem. The outer and inner stems also become discolored from this disorder.

Because the blight actually girdles the tomato stem it prevents it from absorbing water and nutrients, which may cause younger plants to collapse at the soil line.

Septoria leaf spot also produces papery patches on the leaves and is sometimes mistaken for late blight. The leaves also develop tiny, dark specks inside of the leaves with the older leaves affected first.

One of the best ways to handle this problem is through crop rotation. Some experts say that adding extra calcium as well ammonium-containing fertilizers may add an extra bit of protection.

Verticillium wilt is created by a soil-borne fungus and attacks other vegetables, as well as tomatoes. It can kill your plants and is much more pronounced in cool weather.

Symptoms include wilting during the hottest part of day, with recovery at night. There is also yellowing of the leaves with an eventual browning between the leaf veins. The problem starts with the older leaves and produces discoloration inside the stems themselves.

There is not much you can do to fight this one. The most important things you can do are to remove the plants which have been affected.

Then, when choosing plants the following year, be sure to select disease-resistant varieties to give yourself a fighting chance.

The fungus is extremely persistent. It can stay in the soil for years, which makes crop rotation essential, as well as your choice of tomatoes critical.

Spotted wilt virus is a problem more home gardeners are facing today with tomato plants. The disease starts as dark spots on the leaves that quickly spread to the stems, forming cankers. The affected part of the plant then develops a "bronzing" on the leaves.

Once this happens, the growing tips die and the growth of the plant is stunted. If any fruit is produced, it will have yellow spots and rings that form an odd mosaic-like pattern.

Unfortunately, there is no treatment for this particular virus. All infected plants should be discarded and the surrounding area well cleared.

Western Flower Thrip is a virus spread by an insect that is difficult to control. It thrives on weeds; so, it is a good practice to *weed your garden regularly*.

You can also avoid this virus by buying certified virus-free seed and tomato plant varieties which are resistant to it.

If your plants develop a crinkling or a light to dark mottling of the leaves they may be affected by **the tobacco mosaic virus**. When you cut open the fruit from a plant affected by this, you will notice a browning. This disease spreads easily through direct contact with tobacco products.

Actually, it also spreads if your hands have even touched tobacco products. For this reason, if you smoke or handle tobacco products, be sure to wash your hands before you work in your garden.

You can also reduce your exposure to this by choosing plants that are labeled with a T. This indicates that they ds resistant to this particular virus.

Any infected plants or debris must be removed and destroyed to prevent further spreading of the problem.

Being Prepared Is Half the Battle

Now you are a much wiser and more prepared gardener. Vigilant -- that's you. You're ready to protect your tomatoes from just about any form of attack.

Hopefully, you won't have to use much of this material, but it is always good to know.

Our last chapter talks about organic gardening. While you are probably putting many of the following ideas into practice already, it's good to understand some of the essentials of organic farming.

This is especially true if your goal is to take some of those tomatoes to your local farmer's market. Organic produce can offer more than just fruit . . . you may even be able to make some money out of your hobby!

Chapter 6
Growing Organically

So you are thinking about going organic -- even better for your tomatoes and your health!

Growing organic vegetables is a tradition that goes way back . . . do we dare say to the first farmers who planted gardens to help feed their families.

Why Organic?

Many ask that question. If you are growing tomatoes for yourself and your family . . .

> *. . . you will know for sure that the tomatoes you are serving are free of food additives, colorings, or dangerous and poisonous pesticides.*

Market Advantage

Many farmers have a second reason as well. Many of these individuals take their extra fruit into town, to a flea market, or a farmer's market. Organic produce is more profitable because they can charge a little more for their products

Organic tomatoes normally bring 10% to 30% more than conventional tomatoes. If this surprises you then you probably weren't aware that tomatoes are one of the highest pesticide-sprayed vegetables in the world, which explains why there is the potential demand for organically grown tomatoes.

There's a trade-off here as well. If you grow organically instead of conventionally, you'll discover that your crop yield is smaller. However, with today's advances, even that discrepancy is being eliminated.

Where to Begin

Simple, you start by learning the most important rules that every organic farmer follows:

- Careful selection of tomato variety
- Crop rotation
- Soil fertility
- Pest control
- Weed control

Choose Your Tomatoes Wisely

If you've forgotten just how many varieties of tomatoes are available to you, reread the first chapter of this book where we have listed some of the choices. This is only a small fraction of the varieties from which you can choose.

When growing organically, you should **select tomatoes that are as disease-resistant as possible.**

That being said, you also have a second consideration, if you plan to take your crop to the local market. It will do you no good to grow an exotic, high-resistant tomato if no one has really heard of it or the buyers in your area will not appreciate its taste.

Take into account old-fashioned "market demand" Or, you may end up with a lot of extra tomatoes when the growing season ends.

You also need to **consider the climate.** What type of tomato grows well in your area? Remember, weather is always a factor.
You definitely want to avoid a variety that craves heat if you live in northern sections of the country.

When all these factors are carefully considered and fit together as well as possible, your tomatoes will be easier to grow organically and there will be less reason for ever resorting to the use of pesticides.

The Value of Crop Rotation

As an organic farmer, you will quickly learn the value of crop rotation, if you don't already know about it. This means that every year you plant your crops in different areas in your garden from where you planted them the year before.

Efficient organic tomato production means thoughtful rotation.

For example: Don't plant peppers next year where your tomatoes are this year. They are part of the same family, need the same nutrients, and in many instances attract the same pests. Even though it is technically a rotation, you would not be helping the soil or the future fruit crop.

Other plants to avoid rotating with your tomatoes include tobacco, morning glory, and potatoes.

The Importance of Fertile Soil

We talked about this in detail earlier in the book; but, the importance of fertile soil is even more important for organic farmers than for others.

Fortunately, this is not difficult to achieve. Making your soil more fertile requires adding **organic matter** to it on a regular basis.

What exactly is healthy soil?

It is a good balance of water, air, minerals and, of course, organic matter.

Organic matter may sound nice and pristine, but it really isn't either one. It is "plant and animal material in the process of decomposing." It is definitely not pristine.

The Importance of Humus

Once this organic matter has fully decomposed, it's called **humus**. This is essential for the soil because it holds the individual mineral particles together in clusters.

You may have never thought about what "ideal soil" looks like. I certainly never did until I started growing tomatoes, but I quickly learned there is a standard by which all soil is measured.

Ideal soil possesses a granular and even crumbly structure which is perfect for water drainage. The perfect soil structure also allows oxygen and carbon dioxide to freely move between the spaces of the soil and the air above it. *(Never knew there was so much to soil, now did you?)*

One of the best ways to improve your soil – and push it closer to that ideal standard is to add organic matter. This can make the difference between actually growing plump, juicy tomatoes or just watching your neighbor's tomatoes grow them.

Organic Matter Added to Less Than Perfect Soil

If the **soil in your backyard is sandy**, adding organic matter can help it clump and retain water.

If your *soil is more like clay* than anything else, the humus formed by organic matter will help loosen the soil and make it more crumbly (the ideal).

The amount of carbon is the soil is also important because carbon is essential for a successful tomato crop. It promotes the growth of beneficial bacteria, which increases the odds that your plants will be healthy and delicious.

If you are new to organic farming or have soil lacking in certain nutrients, soil preparation (getting it as close to ideal as possible) may be a challenge for you.

Another factor you must consider in soil preparation is making sure it has adequate nitrogen. One way to do this is to rotate your tomato crop with legumes once every few years.

You should also consider adding compost, barnyard manures, and even poultry litter to the soil to help enrich it.

Scientific Evidence on the Benefits of Organic Matter

The scientific community has been researching the benefits of organic matter for years, even decades. An important conclusion they made is that diseases caused by a plant deficiency are usually milder in plants grown organically.

The experts say that organic matter not only increases the health and vigor of the plants, but it affects the behavior of the microbes as well. The organic matter triggers the microbes to be more active.

Specifically, it stimulates friendly microbes to attack and kill the ones that are scouting out your plants. One study revealed that certain types of fungus which live in decaying organic matter have been found to kill harmful nematodes.

Organic Gardening Tip: Put one cup of kelp meal and one cup of bone meal into each planting hole to give them a strong start.

Kelp is rich in micronutrients, and bone meal is rich in phosphorus, which promotes flowers and fruits. They are both slow release fertilizers that provide nutrients over an extended time, rather than all at once. This helps prevent shock, which is a common problem when using chemical fertilizer.

If you like to use "old-timer" tricks, try using one to two tablespoons Epson Salts per hole — when transplanting tomatoes. This provides magnesium, an important plant nutrient.

If you use the above method, be sure to discuss the ongoing fertilizing procedure with an experienced gardener or nurseryman.

NOTE: If you want to focus on organic gardening, look for organic compost and fertilizers. One brand that I can recommend is: <u>*Green Planet.*</u> *They have a good selection at reasonable prices.*

Less Need for Herbicides

As noted earlier, tomatoes are one of the vegetables that are most heavily spayed with harsh chemicals. This is a serious concern for many people – and has become a powerful driver behind the demand for organically grown tomatoes.

It is important to note that organic farmers who follow all the other tenets of the organic approach have less need for herbicides. They simply seem to have fewer pests to worry about; not a bad trade off.

The mere act of practicing crop rotation breaks the life cycle of insects and other pests, and reduces the number of pests that must be controlled.

The Value of Trap Crops

The primary focus of this book is growing tomatoes; however, if you get serious about it over time, you may want to consider growing some trap crops as well.

A good example of a trap crop to grow with your tomato plants is **sweet corn**, for good reason (besides being very tasty).

This particular vegetable attracts the tomato fruit worm, which means than when you plant corn between your rows of tomatoes, the corn will protecting your tomatoes from attack.

Companion Plants

If you are having trouble visualizing corn stalks in your back yard ☺, you may want to consider planting basil instead. This small plant is a delicious herb that serves the same purpose as corn. It is a good example of what is known as a companion plant.

Weed Control

Another hallmark of organic farming involves how the growers deal with controlling the weeds. Weeds are not only a nuisance, they are actually potentially damaging. They can suck up vital nutrients from the soil that your tomatoes need in order to flourish.

Weeds are also a serious source of hidden pests and even diseases. Controlling them through organic means may ultimately save your tomato plants.

Controlling weeds organically means nothing more than using strictly organic material and organic mulches to restrict their growth.

Other good methods of controlling weeds include crop rotation, sanitation and even shallow tilling.

We Live in a Chemical World

It's a fact! You may be aware of the potential problems that pesticides can bring, but many people are not aware. Because of the problem, you need to be very careful about what you put on your plants, including items you may not know about.

If you are interested in growing organically, I am assuming that you do not treat your lawn with chemicals, which is great. But, what about you neighbors? I don't say this casually.

If your neighbor(s) or the HOA spray lawns with chemicals for weed control, it is possible that your plants can be exposed to the chemicals. The spay drifts easily from yard to yard.

Another possible exposure can come from grass clippings that come from chemically sprayed yards. Don't ever use them, even if your neighbor offers.

If the plants are damaged by herbicide, you can tell because the leaves and even the fruit can become distorted. The leaves may bend downward, which causes cupping and thickening.

Some experts believe that catfacing and fruit that doesn't ripen may both be caused by herbicides. So, in addition to the danger that herbicides/pesticides present to the human body, they may also be the source of problems for gardeners who want to grow tomatoes and other produce.

In other words, it is wise to avoid using them, if at all possible.

Without Herbicides, How Do You Get Rid of Pests?

As a tomato gardener, you will encounter a whole host of common garden pests. Creepy critters like cutworms, flea beetles, grasshoppers, spider mites, and root weevils are all too eager to feast on your beautiful, healthy plants.

I couldn't possibly detail how to rid your plants of every insect without using pesticides in one short chapter; but, I can give you information about four of the peskiest pests and suggest some organic solutions.

Controlling Four Common Tomato Pests

Four common tomato pests you will want to guard against are aphids, stink bugs, tomato fruit worms, and flea beetles. The damage these little buggers cause is varied, so it pays to know exactly what you are up against with each.

Let's look at each one and discuss some organic solutions to get rid of them.

Aphids
These tiny green or black insects can be winged or wingless. Either way, they like to hang out in clusters on the bottom side of tomato leaves or tomato stems. They suck moisture and nutrients out of your tomatoes, causing curled and yellowed leaves and stunted plants.

Stink Bugs
True to their name, stink bugs let off a very foul odor if threatened or squashed. Both babies and adults damage your tomatoes by sucking their sap and attacking the fruit.

Young and adult stink bugs look the same with an easily recognized shield-shaped body. Adults can be black, brown or green, with or without markings.

The young ones are basically smaller versions of the adult stink bugs. When they attack your tomatoes, the plants are weakened and young fruit may form improperly as a result.

Yellow-white spots beneath the skin of ripened fruit are a common sign of stink bug damage to your crops.

Tomato Fruit Worms
Also known as the *corn earworm*, these pink, green or brown insects with light striping can grow to nearly two inches long.

They are actually moth larvae that bore into tomato fruit to feed. Moths lay their eggs close to tomato stems with green fruit, and approximately a week later, you will have a tomato fruit worm problem.

Organic Garden Pest Control Solutions

Once you see any of these three common and frustrating tomato pests on your plants, you should take immediate action.

For starters, spray the affected areas with a strong stream of water to dislodge these critters. If you spray several days consecutively, you can eliminate multiple generations of these quickly multiplying pests.

You will also want to employ one of the following organic pest control methods:

1. **Hand picking** – throw on a pair of gardening gloves and fill a large can with warm, soapy water. Then simply pluck the little "darlings" off your plants and drop them into the can.

2. **Weeding** – keep the areas around your plants free from weeds and other garden debris. This eliminates a favorite habitat and hiding place for many garden pests.

3. **Organic insecticidal soap** – mix with water to create a 2% to 3% solution and apply directly to common tomato pests for best results.

4. **Neem oil** – this organic, plant-based oil is very effective against aphids, stink bugs, and tomato fruit worms. You can find it in many garden centers or order it online. Apply according to package directions for best results.

5. **Beneficial insects** – introduce beneficial insects, such as ladybugs, praying mantis, and lacewings (all available for order online) to your garden and let them do what they do best.

Flea beetles

Before we close, let's look at one last little pest, which can also be eliminated without resorting to chemicals.

Their destruction starts with knowing their likes and dislikes.

They like stable, warm spring weather. They dislike alternating periods of cold and hot temperatures that bring intermittent rains.

It is also good to know that seedlings under stress are the most vulnerable to these chewing machines. One of the most stressful situations for a seedling is to be without adequate moisture.

With that information in mind, you want to ensure that your seedlings get adequate nutrition as well as the most favorable growing conditions you can provide – and pay attention so they do not dry out.

By taking these precautions, you will shorten the early growth stages when they are most vulnerable to attack by the beetles.

Many experts believe that using organic fertilizer will make the plants less attractive to the beetles.

Garden pests are an inevitable fact of life for tomato gardeners. However, with a little education and the right resources, you will be able to protect your garden so you can relax and enjoy the fruits of your labors.

Seven Organic Gardening Tips
For Your Best Tomato Crop Ever

If you want to grow the healthiest and most delicious tomatoes you possibly can this gardening season, try implementing the organic gardening tips outlined below.

These are easy-to-implement tricks and tips from the pros that you can use to consistently grow bumper crops of succulent tomatoes.

Many of the points we have covered are included in this list.

1. **Whether growing your tomatoes in containers or in the ground, make sure you select a bright, sunny, and well ventilated, airy location.**
   - Your plants should receive at least 10 hours of natural light in the summer.
   - Also, make sure you have enough room between your tomato plants for adequate air circulation.

2. **Make sure you plant deep for the best possible results**.
   - Burying the stem of a tomato allows the plant to sprout new roots which will help improve strength and vitality.
     - → To do this, remove the bottom sets of leaves and bury the stem up to just below the bottom of the remaining leaves.
     - → This provides better absorption of the nutrients your tomato plants need to grow faster and healthier.
   - You can also plant your tomatoes horizontally in a long trench with just the top leafy part exposed. The plant will correct itself and start growing up vs. along the ground.
     - → Doing this will help your plants establish the strongest root structure possible, because all those little fibers along the plant stem are little roots waiting to develop.

3. **Test your soil - it is crucial for proper tomato growth.**
   - Take a sample of your soil to a nearby gardening or home improvement center that offers lab testing
     - → Or - purchase a DIY pH level testing kit.
   - After you discern the soil's alkaline and acidity levels, you can add the appropriate soil amendments to reach the recommended 6.0 to 6.8 pH for tomatoes.
     - → Most garden centers can tell you just what you need to do to get your soil perfect.

4. **Trick your tomatoes into being stronger by plucking the first flowers that appear.**
   - This allows your tomato plants to grow more extensive root systems, as well as a mature and develop a leaf canopy, before any fruit is produced.
   - You should also pull off any suckers, which are the little offshoots of the main stem below your first fruit-producing branch.

5. **Use cages or fencing to grow your tomatoes vertically**.
   - When you allow tomato vines to lay on the ground, your plants are much more susceptible to pests and diseases.
   - When you provide vertical support, these garden dangers have a harder time attacking your plants.
   - Sprawling vines also take up valuable space in your garden, and the backbreaking process of bending over to harvest the fruit is no fun, either.

6. **When the first fruit of the season begins to appear, add organic compost,** either your own or store bought.
   - Scratch compost into the ground around the stem, and at the same time, trim a few of the upper leaves on each plant.
     - This will encourage new, healthy growth and a bigger yield.

7. **Consider planting another crop of tomatoes three weeks after your original plants are planted.**
    - It extends your growing season
    - It guarantees that if you run into any weather or pest problems, you will still enjoy multiple, healthy harvests.
    - You won't harvest and use your entire crop at once.

Growing tomatoes organically can be a bit more challenging, but well worth the effort. As you harvest your first succulent crop of organically-grown tomatoes you will experience double satisfaction.

- First, you will have the pleasure and enjoyment from the hobby itself.

- Second, you will have peace of mind knowing that at least one type of food you and your family are eating is free from pesticides and other harsh, chemical dangers.

Both are great reasons to give it a try.

Conclusion

Congratulations! You've survived your first season of growing tomatoes. If that doesn't bring you closer to nature . . . nothing will. Plus, I am sure you will agree it is a creative and stimulating way to spend your summer months.

Besides, it's good to know that you can reduce your dependency -- at least a bit -- on your local grocery store. After all, local produce is currently something everyone is talking about . . . from celebrities to authors . . . and everyone in between.

You have been able to contribute to that niche. Even if you didn't sell your produce, you probably shared some of your tomatoes with friends, family and co-workers. I am sure they were quite appreciative.

Whether you continue with this hobby next year is totally up to you. I'm hoping that you enjoyed the experience so much that you can't wait for the next growing season to begin.

I am delighted that I was able to help you learn about growing tomatoes. Hopefully you have enjoyed the time you spent cultivating this new wonderful and worthwhile hobby.

Happy Gardening!

Glossary

Beefsteak: Any of the largest varieties of cultivated tomatoes. They are firm and can weigh up to one pound or more.

Cotyledons: The first or "baby" leaves from the seed of the tomato.

Crack resistant: A type of tomato intentionally bred to resist cracking, a common problem normally caused by sporadic rainfall or excessive rain.

Cultivar: The variety of a plant. Technically, a difference exists between cultivar and "variety." A cultivar is normally viewed as a product of intentional breeding. A variety, by contrast, is considered the product of an accidental cross pollination. However, the two terms are used interchangeably by most growers.

Determinate: A tomato plant whose terminal buds set fruit when plant growth stops. The plant needs little or no staking and the harvest time is short - no more than 10 days.

Heirloom: Generally considered to be a variety of tomato which has been passed through several generations of a family because of specific characteristics. Heirloom varieties have recently gained popularity.

Hybrid pollination: This refers to cross pollination achieved by removing the anthers of parent X before the release of pollen. The Y parent's anther tube is then opened and pollen is removed to be deposited on the stigma of the parent X.

Indeterminate: Plants that continue to grow and produce new blossoms even after fruit sets. The harvest on these plants can last for several months.

Locules: The chambers within the tomato's fruit which hold the seeds within the jelly-like substance. Most fruits have at least two chambers and large fruited varieties can contain up to 10.

Lycopersicon esculentum: The genus and species names for tomato.

Maturity: The number of days from the transplanting of the seedling to the harvesting of the first mature fruit. Early season varieties of tomatoes mature between 55 and 68 days. Midseason varieties mature in 69 to 79 days. Late season take from 80+ days to mature.

Oblate: A slightly flattened, round shape tomato.

Open-pollinated: Seeds from these varieties of tomatoes produce plants and fruit identical to their parent.

Pollination: Pollen grains released by the anther and then fall onto the stigma, usually of the same flower.

Potato leaf: Leaves with no indentations on their margins. So called because they look much like the leaves of the potato plant.

Regular leaf: Leaves with indentations on the leaf margins.

Semi-determinate: Tomato plants larger than the determinate yet smaller than the indeterminate. These usually need staking to grow successfully.

Side-dressing: The act of adding fertilizer around your tomato plants. This is performed upon the initial planting and then several times throughout the year.

Suckers: The name gardeners use for the branches of a tomato plant.

Widely adapted: Refers to any variety of tomato which grows well in more than one growing zone.

Harvesting Tips from
The Old Farmer's Almanac
Since 1872

- Leave your tomatoes on the vine as long as possible. If any fall off before they appear ripe, place them in a paper bag with the stem up and store them in a cool, dark place.

- Never place tomatoes on a sunny windowsill to ripen; they may rot before they are ripe!

- The perfect tomato for picking will be firm and very red in color, regardless of size, with perhaps some yellow remaining around the stem. A ripe tomato will be only slightly soft.

- If your tomato plant still has fruit when the first hard frost threatens, pull up the entire plant and hang it upside down in the basement or garage. Pick tomatoes as they redden.

- Never refrigerate fresh tomatoes. Doing so spoils the flavor and texture that make up that garden tomato taste.

- To freeze, core fresh unblemished tomatoes and place them whole in freezer bags or containers. Seal, label, and freeze. The skins will slip off when they defrost.

Bibliography

"Chapter 1. Introduction." The Importance of Soil Organic Matter. N.p., n.d.
 Web. 10 May 2015.
 <http://www.fao.org/docrep/009/a0100e/a0100e04.htm>.

"Common Tomato Problems." Common Tomato Problems. N.p., n.d. Web.
 15 May 2015.
 <http://www.colostate.edu/Depts/CoopExt/4DMG/Pests/Diseases/tom
 aprob.htm>.

"Crack-Resistant Tomato Varieties - Harvest to Table." *Harvest to Table RSS*.
 N.p., 21 July 2009. Web. 10 May 2015.
 <http://www.harvesttotable.com/2009/07/crack-
 resistant_tomato_varieti/>.

"Efficient Organic Tomato Farming | Organic Facts." Organic Facts. N.p., 02
 Oct. 2007. Web. 12 May 2015. <https://www.organicfacts.net/organic-
 products/organic-cultivation/efficient-organic-tomato-farming.html>.

"Flea Beetle: Organic Control Options." Flea Beetle: Organic Control
 Options. N.p., n.d. Web. 15 May 2015. <https://attra.ncat.org/attra-
 pub/summaries/summary.php?pub=135>.

"Growing Home Garden Tomatoes." G6461. N.p., n.d. Web. 10 May 2015.
 <http://extension.missouri.edu/publications/DisplayPub.aspx?P=G6461
 >.

"Growing Tomatoes from Seed -Technique Tips with Photos." Growing
 Tomatoes from Seed -Technique Tips with Photos. N.p., n.d. Web. 12
 May 2015. <http://www.reneesgarden.com/articles/grow-tomato.htm>.

"Growing Tomatoes in the Home Garden Horticulture Information Leaflet."
 Growing Tomatoes in the Home Garden. N.p., n.d. Web. 30 Apr. 2015.
 <http://content.ces.ncsu.edu/growing-tomatoes-in-the-home-garden/>.

"Harvest Time For Tomatoes: When To Pick Tomatoes." Gardening Know
How. N.p., 14 Aug. 2013. Web. 12 May 2015.
<http://www.gardeningknowhow.com/edible/vegetables/tomato/harve
st-time-for-tomatoes.htm>.

"How to Grow Tomatoes Organically." Common Sense Homesteading. N.p.,
10 Mar. 2014. Web. 10 May 2015.
<http://commonsensehome.com/grow-tomatoes-organically/>.

Iannotti, Marie. "Tomato Plant Leaf Diseases - Gardening Tips." N.p., n.d.
Web. 10 May 2015.
<http://gardening.about.com/od/vegetablepatch/a/TomatoProblems.ht
m>.

Iannotti, Marie. "What Are Cotyledons, Monocots and Dicots?" N.p., n.d. Web.
15 May 2015.
<http://gardening.about.com/od/seedstarting/g/Cotyledons.htm>.

"Information about Catfacing and Growth Cracks." GardenGuides. N.p., n.d.
Web. 30 Apr. 2015. <http://www.gardenguides.com/761-information-
catfacing-growth-cracks-pest-control.html>.

Nardozzi, Charlie. "Chapter 4/Tomatoes: The King of Vegetables."*Vegetable
Gardening for Dummies*. Hoboken, NJ: Wiley, 2009. 42-56. Print.

"National Gardening Association." Food Gardening Guide ::. N.p., n.d. Web. 15
May 2015.
<http://www.garden.org/foodguide/browse/veggie/tomatoes_care/367>.

"The Ohio State University Extension." Blossom-End Rot of Tomato, Pepper,
and Eggplant, HYG-3117-96. N.p., n.d. Web. 12 May 2015.
<http://ohioline.osu.edu/hyg-fact/3000/3117.html>.

"Preparing Your Soil for Planting Tomatoes in the Home Garden." Tomato Dirt. N.p., n.d. Web. 10 May 2015. <http://www.tomatodirt.com/preparing-your-soil.html>.

"Pruning Tomatoes." Fine Gardening. N.p., n.d. Web. 15 May 2015. <http://www.finegardening.com/pruning-tomatoes>.

"Rare, Open-pollinated & Heirloom Garden Seeds." How to Grow Tomatoes from Seed. N.p., n.d. Web. 10 May 2015. <http://www.tomatoseed.com/tomato_growing.html>.

"Tomato | Fruit." Encyclopedia Britannica Online. Encyclopedia Britannica, n.d. Web. 10 May 2015. <http://www.britannica.com/EBchecked/topic/598843/tomato>.

"Tomato Pests & Disease Problems | Tomato Gardening Guru." Planet Natural RSS. N.p., n.d. Web. 5 May 2015. <http://www.planetnatural.com/tomato-gardening-guru/pests-disease/>.

"Tomato Terminology." Tomato Terminology. N.p., n.d. Web. 15 May 2015. <https://www.tomatofest.com/terminology_tomato.html>.

"Tomato Varieties & Color: Learn About Different Tomato Colors." Gardening Know How. N.p., n.d. Web. 5 May 2015. <http://www.gardeningknowhow.com/edible/vegetables/tomato/tomato-varieties-color-learn-about-different-tomato-colors.htm>.

"Tomato Varieties by Color- Yellow Tomatoes - Black Tomatoes - Purple Tomatoes." *Tomato Varieties by Color- Yellow Tomatoes - Black Tomatoes - Purple Tomatoes*. N.p., n.d. Web. 12 May 2015. <http://store.tomatofest.com/Tomato_Varieties_By_Color_s/5.htm>.

"Trellising Your Organic Tomatoes." High Mowing Organic Seeds Blog The
    Seed Hopper. N.p., n.d. Web. 12 May 2015.
    <http://www.highmowingseeds.com/blog/trellising-your-organic-
    tomatoes/>.

"Types of Tomatoes, Tomato Types." Grow Garden Tomatoes. N.p., n.d.
    Web. 12 May 2015. <http://www.growgardentomatoes.com/types-of-
    tomatoes.html>.

Vanderlinden, Colleen. "Open Pollinated, Self Pollinated, Heirloom, Hybrid:
    Definitions." N.p., n.d. Web. 12 May 2015.
    <http://organicgardening.about.com/od/organicgardening101/a/Open-
    Pollinated-Self-Pollinated-And-Hybrid-What-Is-The-Difference.htm>.

"Weather-Related Garden Problems | Horticulture and Home Pest News."
    Weather-Related Garden Problems | Horticulture and Home Pest News.
    N.p., n.d. Web. 10 May 2015.
    <http://www.ipm.iastate.edu/ipm/hortnews/1995/7-21-
    1995/weather.html>.

Whitman, Ann. "Chapter 13/Raising Organic Vegetables." *Organic
    Gardening for Dummies*. Foster City, CA: IDG Worldwide, 2001. 117-18.
    Print.

About the Author

Nancy N. Wilson

All things beautiful are my passion. I enjoy anything that a masterful hand creates - writing, photography, visual arts, cooking, the human body, the human spirit, technology, our beautiful world and so much more.

As a young child, I was very curious and always wanted to know why something worked and how it worked. My mother encouraged me to explore almost anything that interested me. She allowed me to take apart old clocks and radios so that I could figure out how they worked.

The more I learned, the more I wanted to know, which led me quickly to the discovery of the wealth of information available in books, plus the magical journeys I could take through the power of words!

Reading became the center of my life. The town library was located in the Women's Club of the little farming community that I called home. In my eyes, it was the grandest building in town - newly built, with a heavenly air-conditioner that sheltered me from the blazing heat of Arizona summers. It was my personal cocoon in which I could read the hours away.

My first adventure in writing came my senior year in high school when I decided to take a writing correspondence course, which was very forward-looking for the time. I experienced the first thrill of putting pen to paper. It was a magical new adventure! My love affair with the written word began.

Unfortunately, my affair was dealt a serious blow during my first year in college when an English professor told me that I used a lot of words, but said very little. His words went to my very core and hobbled my writing confidence for a number of years. I continued to write, but not with the same excitement and enthusiasm that I had previously enjoyed.

It was not until many years later that everything turned around. After completing my MBA as a "mature woman" I found a position with a Leadership Development Training Company in Manhattan that required use of three of my major passions: my insatiable curiosity of how and why things work, my love of learning through books, and my need to write and be published.

I know, my work was not published in the true sense of the word, but my words were in print and people were reading them and using them to improve their professional lives. I had finally begun to realize my dream.

Now I am retired and living the dream on a daily basis. I write many hours every day. All work is non-fiction. Even though I love fiction, that has never been my focus and there are others who do it so much better than I. My choice has always been, and will continue to be, to write about topics that interest and intrigue me and to share what I discover with my readers.

Other Books by this Author

Cookbooks

Candy Making Made Easy - Instructions and 17 Starter Recipes

Cake Making Made Easy - Instructions and 60 Cakes

Cook Ahead – Freezer to Table

The Healthy Diet Cookbook

Garden Fresh Soups and Stews

Mama's Legacy Series

Seven Volumes Available

Dinner – 55 Easy Recipes (Volume I)

Breakfast and Brunch – 60 Delicious Recipes (Volume II)

Dessert – 50 Scrumptious Choices (Volume III)

Chicken – 25 Classic Dinners (Volume IV)

Mexican Favorites – 21 Traditional Recipes (Volume V)

Side Dish Recipes (Volume VI)

Sauce Recipes – 50 Tasty Choices (Volume VII)

Health and Fitness

DETOX – The Master Cleanse Diet

The Secret to Successful Dieting

Juicing for Life

Business

Attitude Adjustment

A Guide to the Kinstant Formatter

Navigating the Internet Jungle

Books Written Under Pen Names

Everything You Need to Know About Growing Roses

Power Up Your Brain - Five Simple Strategies

All my books can be purchased though my author's page:

http://www.amazon.com/Nancy-N-Wilson

Printed in Great Britain
by Amazon